W9-AER-763

A Book of Sonnets

A BOOK OF SONNETS

edited by

Robert Nye

New York
OXFORD UNIVERSITY PRESS
1976

Printed in Great Britain

Library of Congress Catalog Card Number 75–34887
ISBN 0 19 519841–7

To C. H. Sisson

Contents

Acknowledgements

Permission to use copyright material is gratefully acknowledged to the following:

Faber and Faber Ltd. and Knopf/Random House Inc. for three sonnets from *Collected Shorter Poems* by W. H. Auden; Faber and Faber Ltd. for 'To my Mother' from *Collected Poems 1930–55* by George Barker; Faber and Faber Ltd. and Farrar, Straus and Giroux, Inc. for 'I wished, all the mild days of middle March' from *Berryman's Sonnets* by John Berryman; Oxford University Press for three sonnets from *The Poetical Works of Robert Bridges*; Mr. Alan Hodge and The Hogarth Press for two sonnets from *Collected Poems* by Norman Cameron; Faber and Faber Ltd. for 'Luis De Camoes' from *Talking Bronco* by Roy Campbell; MacGibbon and Kee and Harcourt Brace Jovanovich Inc. for three sonnets from *The Complete Poems* by E. E. Cummings; Carcanet Press for 'Still-Life' from *Collected Poems* by Elizabeth Daryush; the Literary Trustees of Walter de la Mare and The Society of Authors for 'In the Dock' from *The Complete Poems of Walter de la Mare 1969*; William Empson, Harcourt Brace Jovanovich Inc. and Chatto and Windus for 'Camping Out' from *Collected Poems* by William Empson; the Estate of Robert Frost for six sonnets from *The Poetry of Robert Frost* edited by Edward Connery Lathem and published by Holt Rinehart and Winston Inc., and Jonathan Cape Ltd.; Robert Graves and Collins-Knowlton-Wing for 'The Troll's Nosegay' from *Collected Poems 1965* by Robert Graves; the Trustees of the Hardy Estate and Macmillan London, Basingstoke, New York and Canada for six sonnets from *Collected Poems* by Thomas Hardy; John Heath-Stubbs and Oxford University Press for 'Hart Crane' from *Selected Poems* by John Heath-Stubbs; André Deutsch for 'Requiem for the Plantagenet Kings' from *For the Unfallen* by Geoffrey Hill; Oxford University Press for eight sonnets from the fourth edition of poems of Gerard Manley Hopkins edited by W. H. Gardner and N. H. MacKenzie and published by arrangement with the Society of Jesus; Carcanet Press for 'In a Garden' from *Growing-Points* by Elizabeth Jennings; Martin Brian & O'Keeffe for five sonnets by Patrick Kavanagh; Faber and Faber Ltd. and Farrar, Straus and Giroux, Inc. for 'The Card-Players' from *High Windows* by Philip Larkin; Harcourt Brace Jovanovich Inc. for poems by Robert Lowell; Harold Matson Company Inc. for 'Delirium in Vera Cruz' by Malcolm Lowry; Hugh MacDiarmid for 'They Know Not What They Do'; Houghton Mifflin Company for 'The End of the World' from *Collected Poems 1917–1952* by Archibald MacLeish; The Society of Authors as the literary representative of the Estate of John Masefield and Macmillan New York for a sonnet from 'The Pathfinder' by John Masefield; Faber and Faber Ltd. for two sonnets from *Collected Poems 1921–58* by Edwin Muir; Barrie & Rockliffe for 'In negligent stone . . .' by Gil Orlovitz from *Couldn't Say, Might be Love*; the Executors of the Estate of Harold Owen, New Directions, New York and Chatto and Windus for 'Anthem for Doomed Youth' from *The Collected Poems of Wilfred Owen*; Faber and Faber Ltd. and New Directions New York for 'A Virginal' from *Collected Shorter Poems* by Ezra Pound and five sonnets from *The Translations of Ezra Pound*; Knopf/Random House Inc. and Eyre & Spottiswoode Ltd. for 'Piazza Piece' from *Selected Poems* by John Crowe Ransom; Heinemann Educational Books Ltd. for 'Rough Weather' from *Collected Poems 1929–1974* by James Reeves; Carcanet Press Ltd. for 'War and Peace' from *Collected Poems and Translations* by Edgell Rickword; Charles Scribner's Sons for 'George Crabbe', 'Charles Carville's Eyes' and 'Credo' from *The Children of the Night* by Edwin Arlington Robinson; Macmillan New York for 'Many Are Called', 'The Sheaves' and 'New England' from *Collected Poems* by Edwin Arlington Robinson; Iain Crichton Smith for 'Orpheus'; Oxford University Press for 'Sonnets at Christmas' from *The Swimmers and Other Selected Poems* by Allen Tate; J. M. Dent & Sons Ltd. and New Directions, New York for 'When all my five and country senses see' from *Collected Poems* by Dylan Thomas; Hodder and Stoughton Ltd. and A. D. Peters and Co. Ltd. for 'Wordsworth' and 'E.P. at Westminster' from *Nerve Ends* by David Wright; Coward, McCann & Geoghegan Inc. New York for four sonnets from *The Proof* by Yvor Winters; New Directions, New York for 'Sonnet to the moon' from *The Giant Weapon* by Yvor Winters; Knopf/Random House Inc. for 'Wild Peaches' from *Collected Poems of Elinor Wylie*; M. B. Yeats, Miss Anne Yeats and Macmillan Basingstoke, London and New York for 'Leda and the Swan' from *The Collected Poems of W.B. Yeats*.

n the sonnet's argument. It is to be noticed
octave and sestet has disappeared with this
quence that poets writing in it are unlikely to
ught in two units of sense. Instead of the slow
of the Petrarchan sonnet—which is not unlike a
ne shore of consciousness (the octave) and then with-
sestet)—you are presented with what is really a lyric
ree stanzas plus an epigrammatic concluding couplet. It
ident that the Shakespearean mode has proved a favourite
for nnet sequences. A sonnet given this shape may easily be expanded, so that themes and ideas are repeated and each new sonnet thus written becomes as it were a paragraph in the story which is the sequence. (Example: Shakespeare's *They that have power to hurt and will do none*, page 70.)

4. *The Miltonic*: fourteen decasyllabic lines strictly retaining the octave of the Petrarchan sonnet, ABBAABBA, but without any pause—or change of direction—at the beginning of the sestet, which also rhymes in strict accordance with Italian precepts. The effect is like one long wave of words coming in, without any ebb at all. This form lends itself excellently to the single proclamation upon a public theme. The absence of any break between octave and sestet gives the verse movement a sonority and a dignity which Milton exploited to the full, although few have been able to imitate him with success. (Example: *On the Late Massacre in Piedmont*, page 99.)

Each of these forms has something to commend it for specific purposes. The Petrarchan, with its two-part division of the poet's thought, provides a natural ebb and flow of meaning or reflection. The octave gives a unified pattern to the initial deliberation, leading to a turn of thought or change of key or mood at the beginning of the sestet. The Spenserian and Shakespearean sonnets offer relief from the difficulty of rhyming in English. Their movement is swifter, and the opportunity of the couplet has proved useful for poets who like to end a poem with a sting in the tail. The Miltonic sonnet gives a greater unity to the basic Petrarchan form by permitting the octave to run into the sestet, and its long sentence structure suits large verbal gestures made with an air of impersonality. Unlike the other modes the Miltonic has not proved of much use to subsequent poets. You have to take a deep breath and be very sure of your ground to read such a sonnet as *On the Late Massacre in Piedmont* aloud. To write such a sonnet it is necessary to be Milton.

The ebb and flow or cut and thrust of sonnet form, having

Hopkins—not least because he is never too obviously
making a sonnet. You notice first that the thing is a good
then that it follows sonnet form.

That form is defined by the *Oxford English Dictionary* as follows: 'A piece of verse (properly expressive of one main idea) consisting of fourteen decasyllabic lines, with rhymes arranged according to one or other of certain definite schemes.' In French—where Ronsard and Du Bellay were the main exponents of the art of the sonnet in the second half of the sixteenth century—the fourteen lines were usually not decasyllabic at all, but in Alexandrines. In English, however, while the iambic pentameter has been the metrical norm, and excursions into Alexandrines rare, it is the rhyme scheme of the sonnet which has been more variable than is often supposed. The four most common forms to be found in this book may be summarized as follows:

1. *The Petrarchan*: fourteen decasyllabic lines divided into two parts—the first eight lines, called the octave, rhyming ABBAABBA; the remaining six lines, called the sestet, rhyming CDECDE or CDCDCD, or in any similar combination avoiding a closing couplet. Although the rhyme scheme of the sestet admits variations there is never more than a total of five rhymes in a true Petrarchan sonnet. The movement of the poet's mind should be such that the octave puts forward the theme or 'problem' to be developed or examined, while the sestet provides its resolution. (Example: Yvor Winters' *The Castle of Thorns*, page 210.)

2. *The Spenserian*: fourteen decasyllabic lines rhyming ABABB-CBC CDCDEE. This variation, developed by Edmund Spenser, is known also as the 'link' sonnet—because often there is no break between octave and sestet. The epigrammatic final couplet was an English innovation, although not new with Spenser since both Wyatt and Surrey had modified their Petrarchan originals thus. (Example: Spenser's *One day I wrote her name upon the strand*, page 41.)

3. *The Shakespearean*: fourteen decasyllabic lines divided into three quatrains and a concluding couplet. Because of its great prevalence this has also been called the English sonnet, but precisely in view of this it is as well to insist that the Shakespearean sonnet is a native variation on the Petrarchan import. The rhyme scheme is generally ABAB CDCD EFEF GG, or ABBA CDDC EFFE GG. This form was first employed by Wyatt and Surrey during the first half of the sixteenth century, but it was brought to perfection by Shakespeare, who uses the final couplet to express the

 saints and lunar eclipses, a terrier dog, imprisonment in the Tower, buttered pippin-pies, fame, a steam threshing-machine, an army surgeon, a white spider holding a white moth on a white plant, factory-workers, the end of the world, a seat beside the Grand Canal in Dublin, a night nurse going her round, a drunkard smashing a mirror in a South American hotel, a girl cleaning her teeth into a lake, the functional ward of a chest hospital, and Ezra Pound at T. S. Eliot's funeral. Nor is the most extreme material modern or unorthodox—Donne has a sonnet in which he says with perfectly shocking orthodoxy that the Church is most pleasing to God when she behaves like a nymphomaniac, and it is Milton not Auden or E. E. Cummings who rhymes *Tetrachordon* with *what-a-word-on*.

In manner too, the variety of the English sonnet is impressive. George Herbert, Hartley Coleridge, Jones Very, Newman, Clough, and Gerard Manley Hopkins follow the example of Donne's *Holy Sonnets* in finding the form suitable for the exploration of their dealings with the divine. Milton adapts at a stroke the strictest Petrarchan mode to pronounce upon public events and political issues with an authority unrivalled since. Wordsworth sets out to emulate Milton, but finds his purest inspiration in dates outside the history book—as with the sonnet *Composed upon Westminster Bridge, September 3rd, 1802*, 'written on the roof of a coach, on my way to France', when he was going to see what had become of his own hopes regarding the Revolution of 1789, and more particularly what had become of Annette Vallon and his daughter. Keats provides a hectic and unexpected return to the world of Cavalcanti and Petrarch, writing sonnets which are outpourings of doomed passion; but his finest sonnets, like Shelley's, fall outside this mode and are perhaps uncharacteristic—the form helping both poets to achieve something more than the mere expression of personality. Clare stretches the sonnet to make it bear a greater simplicity of utterance, and at the same time shows how the line can be packed with observation of particular natural phenomena. Hardy and Edwin Arlington Robinson use the form as a verse equivalent of the short story. Dylan Thomas carries obscurity further than it will go. Patrick Kavanagh authentically loosens the line to make room for a more conversational tone. Meanwhile, Yvor Winters and Ezra Pound go back to refresh the sonnet at the sources of its formal inspiration. Of these twentieth-century writers, Frost is perhaps the master sonneteer, unobtrusively perfecting a habit of matching turns of common speech to the exigencies of form. He is, in my opinion, the most interesting and inventive technician of the sonnet since

Introduction

The word sonnet comes from the Italian *sonetto*, meaning a little sound or song. Responsibility for invention of the form has been attributed to Pier delle Vigne, secretary of state at the court of the Emperor Frederick II in Sicily. Since Frederick died in 1250, this makes the sonnet one of the oldest shapes in post-classical European poetry. Before being imported into England in the early sixteenth century, the sonnet had been given character as well as form by Italian poets of the Renaissance. Cavalcanti identified it as the rhyming series of sighs associated with neo-Platonic worship of an inaccessible Muse. Dante, by employing the form in the *Vita Nuova*, gave to this worship a theological complexity if not depth. Finally, Petrarch's sequence of sonnets to Laura formalized and summarized the conventions of Courtly Love and imposed coherence upon the pagan and Christian elements in that peculiar activity.

By the time the sonnet arrived in England then, through Wyatt and Surrey and their versions of Petrarch, ideas were already established as to what the thing was and what it might be supposed to do. Once anglicized, however, the sonnet was soon fashioned into something more various, catholic, and robust. This is not surprising, when there were spirits as sceptical as Jonson and Marston to mock its romantic pretensions:

> *His chamber hanged about with elegies,*
> *With sad complaints of his love's miseries;*
> *His windows strewed with sonnets, and the glass*
> *Drawn full of loveknots. I approached the ass,*
> *And straight he weeps, and sighs some sonnet out*
> *To his fair love . . .* (Marston, *Satire III.*)

Shakespeare, whose fair love was a faithless young man and who took his Muse to bed and lived to tell the tale of her bad breath and his self-disgust, may conveniently be celebrated as the point where the *sonetto* becomes the English sonnet. The conceits and languors of Courtly Love are invoked thereafter mostly to be attacked as truthless. *My mistress' eyes are nothing like the sun . . .*

Far from being confined to the musings of yearning suitors and dejected lovers, the English sonnet has accommodated a wide range of subject matter. Thus you will find in this book poems about something in common with the sonata in music, has much to commend it to the general reader of poetry, who can learn in an afternoon where he is with it and then read at his leisure in such a book as this without the difficulty presented by anthologies generally, where each new poem is likely to raise problems of formal definition which confuse or complicate the issue of enjoyment. The fact that the ear expects a certain prescribed sequence of rhymes and is then satisfied in that expectation is one of the things which entitles a fourteen-line verse unit to be called a sonnet. Yet, having summarized the rules, it is only fair to add that the sonnet is not a piece of poetic mathematics but a form of poetic freedom. There are no two first-rate sonnets in the English language which are alike, except in the broad sense of having fourteen decasyllabic lines and rhymes in one or other of the patterns mentioned above. This is because our tongue permits great variety of rhythm within exact metrical limits. You could not find two English poets who write a sonnet in the same way. Personal rhythm cuts across impersonal form.

I have to thank several friends who have helped in the making of this book. First, Mr. Michael Richards, assistant master at the Edinburgh Academy, whose idea of some such book as this inspired the project, and who also helped in the selection and preparation of texts. Then, I am grateful to Miss Elizabeth Jennings, Mr. Anthony Howell, Mr. James Reeves, Mr. Michael Schmidt, Mr. C. H. Sisson, and Mr. David Wright, for the loan of books, for the providing of texts, or for bringing to my notice sonnets which I might otherwise have missed. I am also grateful to the National Library of Scotland where I obtained the great bulk of my texts. Spelling and punctuation have been modernized in the case of the early poets, in the interests of making an anthology which may be read with ease and for pleasure. In the index of contents, titles followed by dots are the first line or part of the first line of a sonnet used as a title; other titles are the poets' own.

ROBERT NYE

Edinburgh
April 1975

Whoso list to hunt, I know where is an hind

Whoso list to hunt, I know where is an hind,
But as for me, *helas!* I may no more.
The vain travail hath wearied me so sore,
I am of them that furthest come behind.
Yet may I, by no means, my wearied mind
Draw from the deer; but as she fleeth afore
Fainting I follow. I leave off therefore,
Since in a net I seek to hold the wind.
Who list her hunt, I put him out of doubt,
As well as I, may spend his time in vain;
And graven with diamonds in letters plain
There is written, her fair neck round about,
"*Noli me tangere*, for Caesar's I am,
And wild for to hold, though I seem tame."

A renouncing of love

Farewell, Love, and all thy laws for ever!
Thy baited hooks shall tangle me no more.
Senec and Plato call me from thy lore
To perfect wealth my wit for to endeavour.
In blind error when I did persever,
Thy sharp repulse, that pricketh aye so sore,
Taught me in trifles that I set no store;
But 'scaped forth thence, since, liberty is lever.
Therefore, farewell! go trouble younger hearts,
And in me claim no more authority.
With idle youth go use thy property,
And thereon spend thy many brittle darts.
For, hitherto though I have lost my time,
Me list no longer rotten boughs to climb.

Divers doth use, as I have heard and know

Divers doth use, as I have heard and know,
  When that to change their ladies do begin,
  To mourn and wail, and never for to lynn,
  Hoping thereby to 'pease their painful woe.
And some there be, that when it chanceth so
  That women change, and hate where love hath been,
  They call them false, and think with words to win
  The hearts of them which otherwhere doth grow.
But as for me, though that by chance indeed
  Change hath outworn the favour that I had,
  I will not wail, lament, nor yet be sad,
Nor call her false that falsely did me feed;
  But let it pass, and think it is of kind
  That often change doth please a woman's mind.

The lover compareth his state to a ship in perilous storm tossed on the sea

My galley, charged with forgetfulness,
Thorough sharp seas in winter nights doth pass
'Tween rock and rock; and eke my foe, alas,
That is my lord, steereth with cruelness;
And every oar a thought in readiness,
As though that death were light in such a case;
An endless wind doth tear the sail apace
Of forced sighs, and trusty fearfulness;
A rain of tears, a cloud of dark disdain,
Hath done the wearied cords great hinderance;
Wreathed with error and eke with ignorance,
The stars be hid that led me to this pain.
  Drowned is reason that should me comfort,
  And I remain, despairing of the port.

I find no peace, and all my war is done

I find no peace, and all my war is done,
I fear, and hope. I burn, and freeze like ice.
I fly above the wind, yet can I not arise.
And naught I have, and all the world I season.
That loseth nor locketh holdeth me in prison,
And holdeth me not, yet can I 'scape nowise:
Nor letteth me live nor die at my devise,
And yet of death it giveth me occasion.
Without eyen I see, and without tongue I 'plain;
I desire to perish, and yet I ask health;
I love another, and thus I hate myself;
I feed me in sorrow, and laugh at all my pain.
  Likewise displeaseth me both death and life,
  And my delight is causer of this strife.

My love took scorn my service to retain

My love took scorn my service to retain:
Wherein me thought she used cruelty,
Since with good will I lost my liberty
To follow her which causeth all my pain.
Might never care cause me for to refrain,
But only this, which is extremity,
Giving me naught, alas, nor to agree
That, as I was, her man I might remain.
But since that thus ye list to order me
That would have been your servant true and fast,
Displease thee not my doting days be past
And with my loss to live I must agree.
  For, as there is a certain time to rage,
  So is there time such madness to assuage.

The pillar perished is whereto I leant

The pillar perished is whereto I leant,
The strongest stay of mine unquiet mind:
The like of it no man again can find,
From East to West still seeking though he went.
To mine unhap for hap away hath rent
Of all my joy the very bark and rind,
And I, alas, by chance am thus assigned
Daily to mourn till death do it relent.
But since that thus it is by destiny,
What can I more but have a woeful heart,
My pen in plaint, my voice in careful cry,
My mind in woe, my body full of smart.
And I myself, myself always to hate,
Till dreadful death do ease my doleful state?

You that in love find luck and abundance

You that in love find luck and abundance
And live in lust and joyful jollity,
Arise for shame! Do away your sluggardy!
Arise, I say, do May some observance!
Let me in bed lie dreaming in mischance;
Let me remember the haps most unhappy
That me betide in May most commonly,
As one whom love list little to advance.
Sephame said true that my nativity
Mischanced was with the ruler of the May;
He guessed, I prove, of that the verity.
In May my wealth and eke my life, I say,
Have stood so oft in such perplexity.
Rejoice! Let me dream of your felicity.

Description of Spring, wherein each thing renews, save only the Lover

The soote[1] season, that bud and bloom forth brings,
With green hath clad the hill and eke the vale,
The nightingale with feathers new she sings;
The turtle to her make[2] hath told her tale.
Summer is come, for every spray now springs;
The hart hath hung his old head on the pale;
The buck in brake his winter coat he flings;
The fishes flete[3] with new-repaired scale;
The adder all her slough away she slings;
The swift swallow pursueth the flies smale;[4]
The busy bee her honey now she mings;[5]
Winter is worn that was the flowers' bale.
  And thus I see among these pleasant things
  Each care decays, and yet my sorrow springs.

Vow to love faithfully, howsoever he be rewarded

Set me whereas the sun doth parch the green,
Or where his beams do not dissolve the ice;
In temperate heat, where he is felt and seen;
In presence prest[6] of people mad or wise;
Set me in high, or yet in low degree;
In longest night, or in the shortest day;
In clearest sky, or where clouds thickest be;
In lusty youth, or when my hairs are gray:
Set me in heaven, in earth, or else in hell,
In hill, or dale, or in the foaming flood;
Thrall, or at large, alive whereso I dwell,
Sick, or in health, in evil fame or good,
  Hers will I be; and only with this thought
  Content myself, although my chance be nought.

[1] sweet [2] mate [3] float [4] small [5] mixes [6] close at hand

I never saw you, madam, lay apart

I never saw you, madam, lay apart
  Your cornet[1] black, in cold nor yet in heat,
  Sith first ye knew of my desire so great,
Which other fancies chased clean from my heart.
Whiles to my self I did the thought reserve,
  That so unware did wound my woeful breast,
  Pity I saw within your heart did rest.
But since ye knew I did you love and serve,
Your golden tress was clad alway in black,
  Your smiling looks were hid thus evermore,
  All that withdrawn that I did crave so sore.
So doth this cornet govern me, alack!
  In summer's sun, in winter breath of frost,
  Of your fair eyes whereby the light is lost.

The fancy, which that I have served long

The fancy, which that I have served long,
That hath alway been enemy to mine ease,
Seemed of late to rue upon my wrong,
And bade me fly the cause of my misease.
And I forthwith did press out of the throng,
That thought by flight my painful flight to please
Some other way, till I saw faith more strong.
And to myself I said, "Alas, those days
In vain were spent, to run the race so long."
And with that thought I met my guide, that plain
Out of the way wherein I wander'd wrong
Brought me amidst the hills in base Bullayne:[2]
Where I am now, as restless to remain,
Against my will, full pleased with my pain.

[1] tall head-dress   [2] Boulogne, where Surrey was engaged in military operations

Th' Assyrian king, in peace, with foul desire

Th' Assyrian king, in peace, with foul desire
And filthy lusts that stained his regal heart;
In war, that should set princely hearts on fire,
Did yield, vanquished for want of martial art.
The dint of swords from kisses seemed strange,
And harder than his lady's side his targe;
From glutton feasts to soldier's fare a change;
His helmet far above a garland's charge:
Who scarce the name of manhood did retain,
Drenched in sloth and womanish delight,
Feeble of spirit, impatient of pain,
When he had lost his honour and his right—
(Proud time of wealth, in storms appalled with dread)—
Murdered himself, to show some manful deed.

Norfolk sprang thee, Lambeth holds thee dead

Norfolk sprang thee, Lambeth holds thee dead,
Clere, of the Count of Cleremont, thou hight.
Within the womb of Ormond's race thou bred,
And sawest thy cousin crowned in thy sight.
Shelton for love, Surrey for lord thou chase;—[1]
Ay me! while life did last that league was tender.
Tracing whose steps thou sawest Kendal blaze,
Landrecy burnt, and battered Bullen[2] render.
At Montreuil gates, hopeless of all recure,
Thine earl, half dead, gave in thy hand his will;
Which cause did thee this pining death procure,
Ere summers four times seven thou couldst fulfill.
Ah, Clere! if love had booted, care, or cost,
Heaven had not won, nor earth so timely lost.

[1] choosest [2] Boulogne

I looked of late and saw thee look askance

I looked of late and saw thee look askance
Upon my door, to see if I sat there,
As who should say: If he be there by chance
Yet may he think I look him everywhere.
No, cruel, no, thou knowest and I can tell
How for thy love I laid my looks aside:
Though thou (percase) hast looked and liked well
Some new-found looks amid this world so wide.
But since thy looks my love have so inchained
That to my looks thy liking now is past,
Look where thou likest, and let thy hands be stained
In true love's blood, which thou shalt lack at last.
 So look, so lack, for in these toys thus tossed,
 My looks thy love, thy looks my life have lost.

You must not wonder though you think it strange

You must not wonder though you think it strange
To see me hold my lowring head so low,
And that mine eyes take no delight to range
About the gleams which on your face do grow.
The mouse which once hath broken out of trap
Is seldom teased with the trustless bait,
But lies aloof for fear of more mishap
And feedeth still in doubt of deep deceit.
The scorched fly which once hath 'scaped the flame
Will hardly come to play again with fire.
Whereby I learn that grievous is the game
Which follows fancy dazzled by desire.
 So that I wink or else hold down my head
 Because your blazing eyes my bale have bred.

That self-same tongue which first did thee entreat

That self-same tongue which first did thee entreat
To link thy liking with my lucky love,
That trusty tongue must now these words repeat,
I love thee still, my fancy cannot move.
That dreadless heart which durst attempt the thought
To win thy will with mine for to consent,
Maintains that vow which love in me first wrought,
I love thee still, and never shall repent.
That happy hand which hardly did touch
Thy tender body to my deep delight,
Shall serve with sword to prove my passion such
As loves thee still, much more than it can write.
  Thus love I still with tongue, hand, heart and all,
  And when I change, let vengeance on me fall.

EDMUND SPENSER

One day I wrote her name upon the strand

One day I wrote her name upon the strand,
  But came the waves and washed it away:
Again I wrote it with a second hand,
  But came the tide and made my pains his prey.
  Vain man (said she), that dost in vain assay
A mortal thing so to immortalise;
  For I myself shall like to this decay,
And eke my name be wiped out likewise.
Not so (quod I); let baser things devise
  To die in dust, but you shall live by fame;
My verse your virtues rare shall eternise,
  And in the heavens write your glorious name:
    Where, whenas death shall all the world subdue,
    Our love shall live, and later life renew.

What guile is this, that those her golden tresses

What guile is this, that those her golden tresses
She doth attire under a net of gold;
And with sly skill so cunningly them dresses,
That which is gold or hair may scarce be told?
Is it that men's frail eyes which gaze too bold,
She may entangle in that golden snare;
And being caught may craftily enfold
Their weaker hearts which are not well aware?
Take heed therefore, mine eyes, how ye do stare
Henceforth too rashly on that guileful net,
In which if ever ye entrapped are,
Out of her bands ye by no means shall get.
Fondness it were for any, being free,
To covet fetters, though they golden be!

Rudely thou wrongest my dear heart's desire

Rudely thou wrongest my dear heart's desire,
In finding fault with her too portly pride:
The thing which I do most in her admire
Is of the world unworthy most envied;
For in those lofty looks is close implied
Scorn of base things, and 'sdain of foul dishonour,
Threatening rash eyes which gaze on her so wide,
That loosely they ne dare to look upon her.
Such pride is praise, such portliness is honour,
That boldened innocence bears in her eyes;
And her fair countenance, like a goodly banner,
Spreads in defiance of all enemies.
Was never in this world ought worthy tried,
Without some spark of such self-pleasing pride.

Men call you fair, and you do credit it

Men call you fair, and you do credit it,
For that yourself ye daily such do see;
But the true fair, that is the gentle wit
And virtuous mind, is much more praised of me.
For all the rest, however fair it be,
Shall turn to nought and lose that glorious hue;
But only that is permanent and free
From frail corruption, that doth flesh ensue.
That is true beauty: that doth argue you
To be divine, and born of heavenly seed;
Derived from that fair Spirit from whom all true
And perfect beauty did at first proceed.
He only fair, and what He fair hath made;
All other fair, like flowers, untimely fade.

Like as a huntsman after weary chase

Like as a huntsman after weary chase
Seeing the game from him escaped away,
Sits down to rest him in some shady place,
With panting hounds beguiled of their prey,—
So, after long pursuit and vain assay,
When I all weary had the chase forsook,
The gentle deer returned the self-same way,
Thinking to quench her thirst at the next brook:
There she beholding me with milder look,
Sought not to fly, but fearless still did bide;
Till I in hand her yet half trembling took,
And with her own good-will her firmly tied.
Strange thing, me seemed, to see a beast so wild
So goodly won, with her own will beguiled.

Happy ye leaves whenas those lily hands

Happy ye leaves whenas those lily hands,
Which hold my life in their dead-doing might,
Shall handle you, and hold in love's soft bands,
Like captives trembling at the victor's sight:
And happy lines, on which with starry light
Those lamping eyes will deign sometime to look
And read the sorrows of my dying sprite,
Written with tears in heart's close bleeding book:
And happy rhymes, bathed in the sacred brook
Of *Helicon*, whence she derived is;—
When ye behold that angel's blessed look,
My soul's long lacked food, my heaven's bliss,
Leaves, lines, and rhymes, seek her to please alone,
Whom if ye please, I care for other none.

This holy season, fit to fast and pray

This holy season, fit to fast and pray,
Men to devotion ought to be inclined:
Therefore I likewise on so holy day
For my sweet Saint some service fit will find.
Her temple fair is built within my mind,
In which her glorious image placed is,
On which my thoughts do day and night attend,
Like sacred priests that never think amiss!
There I to her, as the author of my bliss,
Will build an altar to appease her ire,
And on the same my heart will sacrifice,
Burning in flames of pure and chaste desire:
The which vouchsafe, O Goddess, to accept,
Amongst thy dearest relics to be kept.

Most glorious Lord of life! that on this day

Most glorious Lord of life! that on this day
  Didst make thy triumph over death and sin,
And having harrowed hell didst bring away
  Captivity thence captive, us to win:
  This joyous day, dear Lord, with joy begin;
And grant that we, for whom Thou diddest die,
  Being with thy dear blood clean washed from sin,
May live for ever in felicity,
And that thy love we weighing worthily,
  May likewise love Thee for the same again;
And for thy sake, that all like dear didst buy,
  With love may one another entertain.
    So let us love, dear Love, like as we ought:
    Love is the lesson which the Lord us taught.

SIR WALTER RALEGH

A vision upon the Faery Queen

Methought I saw the grave where Laura lay,
Within that temple where the vestal flame
Was wont to burn; and passing by that way
To see that buried dust of living fame,
Whose tomb fair Love and fairer Virtue kept,
All suddenly I saw the Faery Queen:
At whose approach the soul of Petrarch wept;
And from thenceforth those Graces were not seen,
For they this Queen attended; in whose stead
Oblivion laid him down on Laura's hearse.
Hereat the hardest stones were seen to bleed,
And groans of buried ghosts the heavens did pierce,
  Where Homer's spright did tremble all for grief,
  And cursed the access of that celestial thief.

Like to a hermit poor, in place obscure

Like to a hermit poor, in place obscure,
I mean to spend my days of endless doubt,
To wail such woes as time cannot recure,
Where none but Love shall ever find me out.

My food shall be of care and sorrow made;
My drink nought else but tears fall'n from mine eyes;
And for my light, in such obscured shade,
The flames shall serve which from my heart arise.

A gown of grief my body shall attire;
My staff of broken hope whereon I'll stay;
Of late repentance linked with long desire
The couch is framed whereon my limbs I'll lay.

And at my gate Despair shall linger still,
To let in Death when Love and Fortune will.

Farewell to the Court

Like truthless dreams, so are my joys expired,
And past return are all my dandled days;
My love misled, and fancy quite retired:
Of all which past, the sorrow only stays.

My lost delights, now clean from sight of land,
Have left me all alone in unknown ways;
My mind to woe, my life in Fortune's hand:
Of all which past, the sorrow only stays.

As in a country strange without companion,
I only wail the wrong of death's delays,
Whose sweet spring spent, whose summer well nigh done:
Of all which past, the sorrow only stays:

Whom care forewarns, ere age and winter cold,
To haste me hence to find my fortune's fold.

A secret murder hath been done of late

A secret murder hath been done of late—
Unkindness found to be the bloody knife;
And she that did the deed a dame of state,
Fair, gracious, wise, as any beareth life.

To quit[1] herself, this answer did she make:
Mistrust (quoth she) hath brought him to his end,
Which makes the man so much himself mistake,
To lay the guilt unto his guiltless friend.

Lady, not so. Not feared I found my death,
For no desert thus murdered is my mind.
And yet before I yield my fainting breath,
I quit[2] the killer, though I blame the kind.

You kill unkind; I die, and yet am true—
For at your sight my wound doth bleed anew.

My body in the walls captived

My body in the walls captived
Feels not the wounds of spiteful envy;
But my thrall'd mind, of liberty deprived,
Fast fettered in her ancient memory,
Doth nought behold but sorrow's dying face.
Such prison erst was so delightful
As it desired no other dwelling place,
But time's effects and destinies despiteful
Have changed both my keeper and my fare.
Love's fire and beauty's light I then had store;
But now, close kept, as captives wonted are,
That food, that heat, that light, I find no more.
Despair bolts up my doors, and I alone
Speak to dead walls, but those hear not my moan.

[1, 2] acquit

To his son

Three things there be that prosper up apace
And flourish, whilst they grow asunder far;
But on a day, they meet all in one place,
And when they meet they one another mar:
And they be these—the wood, the weed, the wag.
The wood is that which makes the gallows tree;
The weed is that which strings the hangman's bag;
The wag, my pretty knave, betokeneth thee.
Mark well, dear boy, whilst these assemble not,
Green springs the tree, hemp grows, the wag is wild;
But when they meet, it makes the timber rot,
It frets the halter, and it chokes the child.
  Then bless thee, and beware, and let us pray
  We part not with thee at this meeting day.

JOHN FLORIO

Concerning the honour of books

Since honour from the honourer proceeds,
How well do they deserve, that memorise
And leave in books for all posterities
The names of worthies and their virtuous deeds;
When all their glory else, like water-weeds
Without their element, presently dies,
And all their greatness quite forgotten lies,
And when and how they flourished no man heeds!
How poor remembrances are statues, tombs,
And other monuments that men erect
To princes, which remain in closed rooms
Where but a few behold them, in respect
Of Books, that to the universal eye
Show how they lived; the other where they lie.

With how sad steps, O Moon, thou climb'st the skies

With how sad steps, O Moon, thou climb'st the skies!
How silently, and with how wan a face!
What, may it be that even in heavenly place
That busy archer his sharp arrows tries?

Sure, if that long-with-love-acquainted eyes
Can judge of love, thou feel'st a lover's case;
I read it in thy looks; thy languisht grace
To me that feel the like, thy state descries.

Then, even of fellowship, O Moon, tell me
Is constant love deemed there but want of wit?
Are beauties there as proud as here they be?

Do they above love to be loved, and yet
Those lovers scorn whom that love doth possess?
Do they call virtue there ungratefulness?

Come Sleep, O Sleep! the certain knot of peace

Come Sleep, O Sleep! the certain knot of peace,
The baiting-place of wit, the balm of woe,
The poor man's wealth, the prisoner's release,
The indifferent judge between the high and low;
With shield of proof shield me from out the prease
Of those fierce darts Despair at me doth throw:
Oh, make in me those civil wars to cease!
I will good tribute pay if thou do so.
Take thou of me smooth pillows, sweetest bed,
A chamber deaf to noise and blind of light,
A rosy garland and a weary head:
And if these things, as being thine by right,
Move not thy heavy grace, thou shalt in me
Livelier than elsewhere Stella's image see.

My true love hath my heart, and I have his

My true love hath my heart, and I have his,
By just exchange one for the other given;
I hold his dear, and mine he cannot miss;
There never was a better bargain driven.
His heart in me keeps me and him in one;
My heart in him his thoughts and senses guides;
He loves my heart, for once it was his own;
I cherish his, because in me it bides.
His heart his wound received from my sight;
My heart was wounded with his wounded heart:
For as from me on him his hurt did light,
So still methought in me his hurt did smart.
Both equal hurt, in this change sought one bliss:
My true love hath my heart, and I have his.

Soul's joy, bend not those morning stars from me

Soul's joy, bend not those morning stars from me,
Where Virtue is made strong by Beauty's might;
Where Love is chasteness, Pain doth learn delight,
And Humbleness grows one with Majesty.
Whatever may ensue, O let me be
Co-partner of the riches of that sight;
Let not mine eyes be hell-driv'n from that light;
O look, O shine, O let me die, and see.
For though I oft myself of them bemoan
That through my heart their beamy darts be gone,
Whose cureless wounds even now most freshly bleed,
Yet since my death-wound is already got,
Dear killer, spare not thy sweet-cruel shot;
A kind of grace it is to slay with speed.

Having this day my horse, my hand, my lance

Having this day my horse, my hand, my lance
Guided so well that I obtained the prize,
Both by the judgement of the English eyes
And of some sent from that sweet enemy, France;
Horsemen my skill in horsemanship advance,
Town-folks my strength; a daintier judge applies
His praise to sleight which from good use doth rise;
Some lucky wits impute it but to chance;
Others, because of both sides I do take
My blood from them who did excel in this,
Think Nature me a man of arms did make.
How far they shot awry! The true cause is,
Stella looked on, and from her heavenly face
Sent forth the beams which made so fair my race.

No more, my dear, no more these counsels try

No more, my dear, no more these counsels try;
O give my passions leave to run their race!
Let Fortune lay on me her worst disgrace,
Let folk o'ercharged with brain against me cry;
Let clouds bedim my face, break in mine eye,
Let me no steps but of lost labour trace;
Let all the earth with scorn recount my case;
But do not will me from my love to fly.
I do not envy Aristotle's wit,
Nor do aspire to Caesar's bleeding fame;
Nor ought do care though some above me sit;
Nor hope nor wish another course to frame,
But that which once may win thy cruel heart:
Thou art my wit, and thou my virtue art.

Thou blind man's mark, thou fool's self-chosen snare

Thou blind man's mark, thou fool's self-chosen snare,
Fond fancy's scum, and dregs of scattered thought;
Band of all evils, cradle of causeless care;
Thou web of will, whose end is never wrought:
Desire! Desire! I have too dearly bought,
With price of mangled mind, thy worthless ware;
Too long, too long, asleep thou hast me brought,
Who shouldst my mind to higher things prepare.
But yet in vain thou hast my ruin sought,
In vain thou mad'st me to vain things aspire,
In vain thou kindlest all thy smoke fire,
For Virtue hath this better lesson taught:
Within myself to seek my only hire,
Desiring nought but how to kill Desire.

Because I breathe not love to every one

Because I breathe not love to every one,
Nor do not use set colours for to wear,
Nor nourish special locks of vowed hair,
Nor give each speech a full point of a groan,
The courtly nymphs, acquainted with the moan
Of them who in their lips Love's standard bear:
'What, he!' say they of me: 'now I dare swear
He cannot love. No, no, let him alone.'—
And think so still, so Stella know my mind!
Profess indeed I do not Cupid's art;
But you, fair maids, at length this true shall find,
That his right badge is but worn in the heart:
Dumb swans, not chattering pies,[1] do lovers prove;
They love indeed who quake to say they love.

[1] magpies

Loving in truth, and fain in verse my love to show

Loving in truth, and fain in verse my love to show,
That she, dear she, might take some pleasure of my pain:
Pleasure might cause her read, reading might make her know,
Knowledge might pity win, and pity grace obtain,—
I sought fit words to paint the blackest face of woe,
Studying inventions fine, her wits to entertain,
Oft turning others' leaves, to see if thence would flow
Some fresh and fruitful showers upon my sun-burn'd brain.

But words came halting forth, wanting Invention's stay;
Invention, Nature's child, fled step-dame Study's blows;
And others' feet still seemed but strangers in my way.
Thus, great with child to speak, and helpless in my throes,
Biting my truant pen, beating myself for spite;
Fool, said my Muse to me, look in thy heart, and write!

Leave me, O Love, which reachest but to dust

Leave me, O Love, which reachest but to dust;
And thou my mind aspire to higher things;
Grow rich in that which never taketh rust:
Whatever fades, but fading pleasure brings.

Draw in thy beams, and humble all thy might
To that sweet yoke where lasting freedoms be,
Which breaks the clouds and opens forth the light
That doth both shine and give us sight to see.

O, take fast hold! let that light be thy guide
In this small course which birth draws out to death,
And think how evil becometh him to slide
Who seeketh heaven, and comes of heavenly breath.
Then farewell, world; thy uttermost I see:
Eternal Love, maintain thy life in me.

The nurse-life wheat, within his green husk growing

The nurse-life[1] wheat, within his green husk growing,
Flatters our hope, and tickles our desire,
Nature's true riches in sweet beauties showing,
Which set all hearts, with labour's love, on fire.

No less fair is the wheat when golden ear
Shows unto hope the joys of near enjoying:
Fair and sweet is the bud, more sweet and fair
The rose, which proves that time is not destroying.

Caelica, your youth, the morning of delight,
Enamelled o'er with beauties white and red,
All sense and thoughts did to belief invite,
That love and glory there are brought to bed;
And your ripe years love none; he goes no higher,
Turns all the spirits of man into desire.

Cupid, thou naughty boy, when thou wert loathed

Cupid, thou naughty boy, when thou wert loathed,
Naked and blind, for vagabonding noted,
Thy nakedness I with my reason clothed,
Mine eyes I gave thee, so was I devoted.

Fie, wanton, fie; who would show children kindness?
No sooner he into mine eyes was gotten
But straight he clouds them with a seeing blindness,
Makes reason wish that reason were forgotten.

From thence to Myra's eyes the wanton strayeth,
Where, while I charge him with ungrateful measure,
So with fair wonders he mine eyes betrayeth,
That my wounds, and his wrongs, become my pleasure;
Till for more spite to Myra's heart he flieth,
Where, living to the world, to me he dieth.

[1] life-fostering

Satan, no woman, yet a wandering spirit

Satan, no woman, yet a wandering spirit,
When he saw ships sail two ways with one wind,
Of sailors' trade he hell did disinherit:
The Devil himself loves not a half-fast mind.

The satyr when he saw the shepherd blow
To warm his hands, and make his pottage cool,
Manhood forswears, and half a beast did know,
Nature with double breath is put to school.

Cupid doth head his shafts in women's faces,
Where smiles and tears dwell ever near together,
Where all the arts of change give passion graces;
While these clouds threaten, who fears not the weather?
Sailors and satyrs, Cupid's knights, and I,
Fear women that swear, Nay; and know they lie.

In night when colours all to black are cast

In night when colours all to black are cast,
Distinction lost, or gone down with the light;
The eye a watch to inward senses plac'd,
Not seeing, yet still having power of sight,
Gives vain alarums to the inward sense,
Where fear stirr'd up with witty tyranny,
Confounds all powers, and thorough self-offence,
Doth forge and raise impossibility:
Such is in thick depriving darknesses,
Proper reflections of the error be,
And images of self-confusednesses,
Which hurt imaginations only see;
And from this nothing seen, tells news of devils,
Which but expressions be of inward evils.

Muses that sing Love's sensual empery

Muses that sing Love's sensual empery,
And lovers kindling your enraged fires
At Cupid's bonfires burning in the eye,
Blown with the empty breath of vain desires,—
You that prefer the painted cabinet
Before the wealthy jewels it doth store ye,
That all your joys in dying figures set,
And stain the living substance of your glory;
Abjure those joys, abhor their memory,
And let my Love the honoured subject be
Of love, and honour's complete history;
Your eyes were never yet let in to see
The majesty and riches of the mind,
But dwell in darkness; for your god is blind.

ROBERT GREENE

Reason, that long in prison of my will

Reason, that long in prison of my will
Hast wept thy mistress' wants and loss of time,
Thy wonted siege of honour safely climb;
To thee I yield as guilty of mine ill.
Lo, fettered in their tears, mine eyes are prest
To pay due homage to their native guide:
My wretched heart, wounded with bad betide,
To crave his peace from reason is addrest.
My thoughts ashamed, since by themselves consumed,
Have done their duty to repentance wit:
Ashamed of all, sweet guide, I sorry sit,
To see in youth how I too far presumed.
Thus he whom love and error did betray
Subscribes to thee and takes the better way.

What meant the poets in invective verse

What meant the poets in invective verse
To sing Medea's shame, and Scylla's pride,
Calypso's charms by which so many died?
Only for this their vices they rehearse:
That curious wits which in the world converse,
May shun the dangers and enticing shows
Of such false sirens, those home-breeding foes,
That from their eyes their venom do disperse.
So soon kills not the basilisk with sight;
The viper's tooth is not so venomous;
The adder's tongue not half so dangerous,
As they that bear the shadow of delight,
Who chain blind youths in trammels of their hair,
Till waste brings woe, and sorrow hastes despair.

HENRY CONSTABLE

To St Michael the Archangel

When as the prince of angels, puff'd with pride
  Stirred his seditious spirits to rebel,
  God chose for chief his Champion Michael,
  And gave him charge the host of heaven to guide.
And when the angels of the rebels' side
  Vanquished in battle from their glory fell,
  The pride of heaven became the drake of hell
  And in the dungeon of despair was tied.
This dragon, since let loose, God's Church assail'd,
  And she, by help of Michael's sword, prevailed.
  Who ever tried adventures like this Knight
Which, general of heaven, hell o'erthrew;
  For such a lady as God's spouse did fight,
  And such a monster as the devil subdue?

To St Katharine

Because thou wast the daughter of a king,
Whose beauty did all Nature's works exceed,
And wisdom wonder to the world did breed,
A muse might rouse itself on Cupid's wing;
But, sith the graces which from nature spring
Were graced by those which from grace did proceed,
And glory have deserved, my Muse doth need
An angel's feathers when thy praise I sing.
For all in thee became angelical:
An angel's face had angels' purity,
And thou an angel's tongue didst speak withal;
Lo! why thy soul, set free by martyrdom,
Was crowned by God in angels' company,
And angels' hands thy body did entomb.

Of his mistress, upon occasion of her walking in a garden

My lady's presence makes the roses red,
Because to see her lips they blush for shame:
The lily's leaves, for envy, pale became,
And her white hands in them this envy bred.
The marigold abroad her leaves doth spread,
Because the sun's and her power is the same;
The violet of purple colour came,
Dyed with the blood she made my heart to shed.
In brief, all flowers from her their virtue take:
From her sweet breath their sweet smells do proceed,
The living heat which her eye-beams do make
Warmeth the ground, and quickeneth the seed.
The rain wherewith she watereth these flowers
Falls from mine eyes, which she dissolves in showers.

Needs must I leave, and yet needs must I love

Needs must I leave, and yet needs must I love;
In vain my wit doth paint in verse my woe:
Disdain in thee despair in me doth show
How by my wit I do my folly prove.
All this my heart from love can never move;
Love is not in my heart, no, lady, no:
My heart is love itself; till I forego
My heart, I never can my love remove.
How shall I then leave love? I do intend
Not to crave grace, but yet to wish it still;
Not to praise thee, but beauty to commend,
And so by beauty's praise, praise thee I will.
For as my heart is love, love not in me,
So beauty thou,—beauty is not in thee.

Pity refusing my poor Love to feed

Pity refusing my poor Love to feed,
A beggar starved for want of help he lies,
And at your mouth, the door of beauty, cries
That thence some alms of sweet grants may proceed.
But as he waiteth for some alms-deed,
A cherry-tree before the door he spies—
'O dear!' quoth he, 'two cherries may suffice,
Two only life may save in this my need.'
But beggars, can they nought but cherries eat?
Pardon my Love, he is a goddess' son,
And never feedeth but on dainty meat,
Else need he not to pine as he hath done:
For only the sweet fruit of this sweet tree
Can give food to my Love, and life to me.

Look, Delia, how w' esteem the half-blown rose

Look, Delia, how w' esteem the half-blown rose,
The image of thy blush and summer's honour,
Whilst yet her tender bud doth undisclose
That full of beauty Time bestows upon her.
No sooner spreads her glory in the air,
But straight her wide-blown pomp comes to decline;
She then is scorned that late adorned the fair;
So fade the roses of those cheeks of thine.
No April can revive thy withered flowers,
Whose springing grace adorns thy glory now;
Swift speedy Time, feathered with flying hours,
Dissolves the beauty of the fairest brow.
  Then do not thou such treasure waste in vain,
  But love now whilst thou mayst be loved again.

Care-charmer Sleep, son of the sable Night

Care-charmer Sleep, son of the sable Night,
Brother to Death, in silent darkness born,
Relieve my languish, and restore the light;
With dark forgetting of my care return,
And let the day be time enough to mourn
The shipwreck of my ill-adventured youth:
Let waking eyes suffice to wail their scorn,
Without the torment of the night's untruth.
Cease, dreams, the images of day-desires,
To model forth the passions of the morrow;
Never let rising Sun approve you liars,
To add more grief to aggravate my sorrow:
  Still let me sleep, embracing clouds in vain,
  And never wake to feel the day's disdain.

Since there's no help, come let us kiss and part

Since there's no help, come let us kiss and part,—
Nay I have done, you get no more of me;
And I am glad, yea glad with all my heart,
That thus so cleanly I myself can free;
Shake hands for ever, cancel all our vows,
And when we meet at any time again,
Be it not seen in either of our brows
That we one jot of former love retain.
Now at the last gasp of Love's latest breath,
When, his pulse failing, Passion speechless lies,
When Faith is kneeling by his bed of death,
And Innocence is closing up his eyes,—
Now if thou would'st, when all have given him over,
From death to life thou might'st him yet recover!

My thoughts bred up with Eagle-birds of Jove

My thoughts bred up with Eagle-birds of Jove,
And, for their virtues I desired to know,
Upon the nest I set them forth, to prove
If they were of the Eagles kind or no:
But they no sooner saw my Sun appear,
But on her rays with gazing eyes they stood;
Which proved my birds delighted in the air,
And that they came of this rare kingly brood.
But now their plumes, full sumd with sweet desire,
To shew their kind began to climb the skies:
Do what I could my Eaglets would aspire,
Straight mounting up to thy celestial eyes.
And thus (my fair) my thoughts away be flown,
And from my breast into thine eyes be gone.

How many paltry, foolish, painted things

How many paltry, foolish, painted things,
That now in coaches trouble every street,
Shall be forgotten, whom no poet sings,
Ere they be well wrapped in their winding-sheet?
Where I to thee eternity shall give,
When nothing else remaineth of these days,
And Queens hereafter shall be glad to live
Upon the alms of thy superfluous praise.
Virgins and matrons, reading these my rhymes,
Shall be so much delighted with thy story,
That they shall grieve they lived not in these times,
To have seen thee, their sex's only glory.
So shalt thou fly above the vulgar throng,
Still to survive in my immortal song.

As Love and I, late harbour'd in one Inn

As Love and I, late harbour'd in one Inn,
With proverbs thus each other entertain,
In love there is no lack, thus I begin;
Fair words make fools, replieth he again;
That spares to speak doth spare to speed, quoth I,
As well, saith he, *too forward as too slow*:
Fortune assists the boldest, I reply;
A hasty man, quoth he, *ne'er wanted woe*.
Labour is light where love, quoth I, *doth pay*;
Saith he, *Light burden's heavy, if far borne*:
Quoth I, *The main lost, throw the bye away*;
You have spun a fair thread, he replies in scorn.
And having thus awhile each other thwarted,
Fools as we met, so fools again we parted.

JOSHUA SYLVESTER

Were I as base as is the lowly plain

Were I as base as is the lowly plain,
And you, my Love, as high as heaven above,
Yet should the thoughts of me your humble swain
Ascend to heaven in honour of my Love.
Were I as high as heaven above the plain,
And you, my Love, as humble and as low
As are the deepest bottoms of the main,
Whereso'er you were, with you my love should go.
Were you the earth, dear Love, and I the skies,
My Love should shine on you like to the sun,
And look upon you with ten thousand eyes,
Till heaven waxed blind, and till the world were done.
Whereso'er I am, below or else above you,
Whereso'er you are, my heart shall truly love you.

MARK ALEXANDER BOYD

Fra bank to bank, fra wood to wood I rin

Fra bank to bank, fra wood to wood I rin,
  Ourhailit with my feeble fantasie;
  Like til a leaf that fallis from a tree,
Or til a reed ourblawin with the win.

Twa gods guides me: the ane of tham is blin,
  Yea and a bairn brocht up in vanitie;
  The next a wife ingenrit of the sea,
And lichter nor a dauphin with her fin.

Unhappy is the man for evermair
That tills the sand and sawis in the air;
  But twice unhappier is he, I lairn,
That feidis in his hairt a mad desire,
And follows on a woman throw the fire,
  Led by a blind and teachit by a bairn.

To the moon

Look how the pale queen of the silent night
  Doth cause the Ocean to attend upon her,
And he, as long as she is in his sight,
  With his full tide is ready her to honour;
But when the silver waggon of the Moon
  Is mounted up so high he cannot follow,
The sea calls home his crystal waves to moan,
  And with low ebb doth manifest his sorrow.
So you, that are the sovereign of my heart,
  Have all my joys attending on your will,
My joys low-ebbing when you do depart—
  When you return, their tide my heart doth fill:
    So as you come, and as you do depart,
    Joys ebb and flow within my tender heart.

WILLIAM SHAKESPEARE

Shall I compare thee to a summer's day

Shall I compare thee to a summer's day?
Thou art more lovely and more temperate:
Rough winds do shake the darling buds of May,
And summer's lease hath all too short a date:
Sometime too hot the eye of heaven shines,
And often is his gold complexion dimm'd;
And every fair from fair sometime declines,
By chance, or nature's changing course, untrimm'd;
But thy eternal summer shall not fade,
Nor lose possession of that fair thou ow'st;
Nor shall Death brag thou wand'rest in his shade,
When in eternal lines to time thou grow'st:
  So long as men can breathe, or eyes can see,
  So long lives this, and this gives life to thee.

When, in disgrace with fortune and men's eyes

When, in disgrace with fortune and men's eyes,
I all alone beweep my outcast state,
And trouble deaf heaven with my bootless cries,
And look upon myself, and curse my fate,
Wishing me like to one more rich in hope,
Featured like him, like him with friends possest,
Desiring this man's art, and that man's scope,
With what I most enjoy contented least;
Yet in these thoughts myself almost despising,
Haply I think on thee, and then my state,
Like to the lark at break of day arising
From sullen earth, sings hymns at heaven's gate;
For thy sweet love rememb'red such wealth brings
That then I scorn to change my state with kings.

Full many a glorious morning have I seen

Full many a glorious morning have I seen
Flatter the mountain-tops with sovereign eye,
Kissing with golden face the meadows green,
Gilding pale streams with heavenly alchemy;
Anon permit the basest clouds to ride
With ugly rack on his celestial face,
And from the forlorn world his visage hide,
Stealing unseen to west with this disgrace:
Even so my sun one early morn did shine
With all-triumphant splendour on my brow;
But, out, alack! he was but one hour mine,
The region cloud hath maskt him from me now.
Yet him for this my love no whit disdaineth;
Suns of the world may stain when heaven's sun staineth.

No more be grieved at that which thou hast done

No more be grieved at that which thou hast done:
Roses have thorns, and silver fountains mud;
Clouds and eclipses stain both moon and sun,
And loathsome canker lives in sweetest bud.
All men make faults, and even I in this,
Authorizing thy trespass with compare,
Myself corrupting, salving thy amiss,
Excusing their sins more than thy sins are;
For to thy sensual fault I bring in sense,—
Thy adverse party is thy advocate,—
And 'gainst myself a lawful plea commence:
Such civil war is in my love and hate,
  That I an accessary needs must be
  To that sweet thief which sourly robs from me.

If the dull substance of my flesh were thought

If the dull substance of my flesh were thought,
Injurious distance should not stop my way;
For then, despite of space, I would be brought,
From limits far remote, where thou dost stay.
No matter then although my foot did stand
Upon the farthest earth removed from thee;
For nimble thought can jump both sea and land,
As soon as think the place where he would be.
But, ah, thought kills me, that I am not thought,
To leap large lengths of miles when thou art gone,
But that, so much of earth and water wrought,
I must attend time's leisure with my moan;
  Receiving naught by elements so slow
  But heavy tears, badges of either's woe.

Not marble, nor the gilded monuments

Not marble, nor the gilded monuments
Of princes, shall outlive this powerful rime;
But you shall shine more bright in these contents
Than unswept stone, besmear'd with sluttish time.
When wasteful war shall statues overturn,
And broils root out the work of masonry,
Nor Mars his sword nor war's quick fire shall burn
The living record of your memory.
'Gainst death and all-oblivious enmity
Shall you pace forth; your praise shall still find room
Even in the eyes of all posterity
That wear this world out to the ending doom.
So, till the judgement that yourself arise,
You live in this, and dwell in lovers' eyes.

Sin of self-love possesseth all mine eye

Sin of self-love possesseth all mine eye,
And all my soul, and all my every part;
And for this sin there is no remedy,
It is so grounded inward in my heart.
Methinks no face so gracious is as mine,
No shape so true, no truth of such account;
And for myself mine own worth do define,
As I all other in all worths surmount.
But when my glass shows me myself indeed,
Beated and chopt with tann'd antiquity,
Mine own self-love quite contrary I read;
Self so self-loving were iniquity.
'Tis thee, myself, that for myself I praise,
Painting my age with beauty of thy days.

Since brass, nor stone, nor earth, nor boundless sea

Since brass, nor stone, nor earth, nor boundless sea,
But sad mortality o'ersways their power,
How with this rage shall beauty hold a plea,
Whose action is no stronger than a flower?
O, how shall summer's honey breath hold out
Against the wrackful siege of battering days,
When rocks impregnable are not so stout,
Nor gates of steel so strong, but Time decays?
O fearful meditation! where, alack,
Shall Time's best jewel from Time's chest lie hid?
Or what strong hand can hold his swift foot back?
Or who his spoil of beauty can forbid?
  O, none, unless this miracle have might,
  That in black ink my love may still shine bright.

Tired with all these, for restful death I cry

Tired with all these, for restful death I cry,—
As, to behold Desert a beggar born,
And needy Nothing trimm'd in jollity,
And purest Faith unhappily forsworn,
And gilded Honour shamefully misplaced,
And maiden Virtue rudely strumpeted,
And right Perfection wrongfully disgraced,
And Strength by limping Sway disabled,
And Art made tongue-tied by Authority,
And Folly, doctor-like, controlling Skill,
And simple Truth miscall'd Simplicity,
And captive Good attending captain Ill:
  Tired with all these, from these would I be gone,
  Save that, to die, I leave my love alone.

No longer mourn for me when I am dead

No longer mourn for me when I am dead
Than you shall hear the surly sullen bell
Give warning to the world that I am fled
From this vile world, with vilest worms to dwell:
Nay, if you read this line, remember not
The hand that writ it; for I love you so,
That I in your sweet thoughts would be forgot,
If thinking on me then should make you woe.
O, if, I say, you look upon this verse
When I perhaps compounded am with clay,
Do not so much as my poor name rehearse,
But let your love even with my life decay;
  Lest the wise world should look into your moan,
  And mock you with me after I am gone.

That time of year thou mayst in me behold

That time of year thou mayst in me behold
When yellow leaves, or none, or few, do hang
Upon those boughs which shake against the cold,
Bare ruin'd choirs where late the sweet birds sang.
In me thou see'st the twilight of such day
As after sunset fadeth in the west;
Which by and by black night doth take away,
Death's second self, that seals up all in rest.
In me thou see'st the glowing of such fire
That on the ashes of his youth doth lie,
As the death-bed whereon it must expire,
Consumed with that which it was nourisht by.
  This thou perceivest, which makes thy love more strong,
  To love that well which thou must leave ere long.

Farewell! thou art too dear for my possessing

Farewell! thou art too dear for my possessing,
And like enough thou know'st thy estimate:
The charter of thy worth gives thee releasing:
My bonds in thee are all determinate.
For how do I hold thee but by thy granting?
And for that riches where is my deserving?
The cause of this fair gift in me is wanting,
And so my patent back again is swerving.
Thyself thou gavest, thy own worth then not knowing,
Or me, to whom thou gavest it, else mistaking;
So thy great gift, upon misprision growing,
Comes home again, on better judgement making.
  Thus have I had thee, as a dream doth flatter,
  In sleep a king, but waking no such matter.

They that have power to hurt and will do none

They that have power to hurt and will do none,
That do not do the thing they most do show,
Who, moving others, are themselves as stone,
Unmoved, cold, and to temptation slow;
They rightly do inherit heaven's graces,
And husband nature's riches from expense;
They are the lords and owners of their faces,
Others but stewards of their excellence.
The summer's flower is to the summer sweet,
Though to itself it only live and die;
But if that flower with base infection meet,
The basest weed outbraves his dignity:
  For sweetest things turn sourest by their deeds;
  Lilies that fester smell far worse than weeds.

From you have I been absent in the spring

From you have I been absent in the spring,
When proud-pied April, drest in all his trim,
Hath put a spirit of youth in every thing,
That heavy Saturn laught and leapt with him.
Yet nor the lays of birds, nor the sweet smell
Of different flowers in odour and in hue,
Could make me any summer's story tell,
Or from their proud lap pluck them where they grew:
Nor did I wonder at the lily's white,
Nor praise the deep vermilion in the rose;
They were but sweet, but figures of delight,
Drawn after you,—you pattern of all those.
  Yet seem'd it winter still, and, you away,
  As with your shadow I with these did play.

When in the chronicle of wasted time

When in the chronicle of wasted time
I see descriptions of the fairest wights,
And beauty making beautiful old rime
In praise of ladies dead and lovely knights,
Then, in the blazon of sweet beauty's best,
Of hand, of foot, of lip, of eye, of brow,
I see their antique pen would have exprest
Even such a beauty as you master now.
So all their praises are but prophecies
Of this our time, all you prefiguring;
And, for they lookt but with divining eyes,
They had not skill enough your worth to sing:
  For we, which now behold these present days,
  Have eyes to wonder, but lack tongues to praise.

Not mine own fears, nor the prophetic soul

Not mine own fears, nor the prophetic soul
Of the wide world dreaming on things to come,
Can yet the lease of my true love control,
Supposed as forfeit to a confined doom.
The mortal moon hath her eclipse endured,
And the sad augurs mock their own presage;
Incertainties now crown themselves assured,
And peace proclaims olives of endless age.
Now with the drops of this most balmy time
My love looks fresh, and Death to me subscribes,
Since, spite of him, I'll live in this poor rime,
While he insults o'er dull and speechless tribes:
  And thou in this shalt find thy monument,
  When tyrants' crests and tombs of brass are spent.

Let me not to the marriage of true minds

Let me not to the marriage of true minds
Admit impediments. Love is not love
Which alters when it alteration finds,
Or bends with the remover to remove:
O, no! it is an ever-fixed mark,
That looks on tempests and is never shaken;
It is the star to every wand'ring bark,
Whose worth's unknown, although his height be taken.
Love's not Time's fool, though rosy lips and cheeks
Within his bending sickle's compass come;
Love alters not with his brief hours and weeks,
But bears it out even to the edge of doom.
  If this be error, and upon me proved,
  I never writ, nor no man ever loved.

That you were once unkind befriends me now

That you were once unkind befriends me now,
And for that sorrow which I then did feel
Needs must I under my transgression bow,
Unless my nerves were brass or hammer'd steel.
For if you were by my unkindness shaken,
As I by yours, y'have past a hell of time;
And I, a tyrant have no leisure taken
To weigh how once I suffer'd in your crime.
O, that our night of woe might have rememb'red
My deepest sense, how hard true sorrow hits,
And soon to you, as you to me then, tend'red
The humble salve which wounded bosom fits!
  But that, your trespass, now becomes a fee;
  Mine ransoms yours, and yours must ransom me.

'Tis better to be vile than vile esteemed

'Tis better to be vile than vile esteemed,
When not to be receives reproach of being;
And the just pleasure lost, which is so deemed
Not by our feeling, but by others' seeing:
For why should others' false adulterate eyes
Give salutation to my sportive blood?
Or on my frailties why are frailer spies,
Which in their wills count bad what I think good?
No, I am that I am; and they that level
At my abuses reckon up their own:
I may be straight, though they themselves be bevel;
By their rank thoughts my deeds must not be shown;
  Unless this general evil they maintain—
  All men are bad, and in their badness reign.

How oft, when thou, my music, music play'st

How oft, when thou, my music, music play'st,
Upon that blessed wood whose motion sounds
With thy sweet fingers, when thou gently sway'st
The wiry concord that mine ear confounds,
Do I envy those jacks that nimble leap
To kiss the tender inward of thy hand,
Whilst my poor lips, which should that harvest reap,
At the wood's boldness by thee blushing stand!
To be so tickled, they would change their state
And situation with those dancing chips,
O'er whom thy fingers walk with gentle gait,
Making dead wood more blest than living lips.
  Since saucy jacks so happy are in this,
  Give them thy fingers, me thy lips to kiss.

Th' expense of spirit in a waste of shame

Th' expense of spirit in a waste of shame
Is lust in action; and till action, lust
Is perjured, murd'rous, bloody, full of blame,
Savage, extreme, rude, cruel, not to trust;
Enjoy'd no sooner but despised straight;
Past reason hunted; and no sooner had,
Past reason hated, as a swallow'd bait,
On purpose laid to make the taker mad:
Mad in pursuit, and in possession so;
Had, having, and in quest to have, extreme;
A bliss in proof, and proved, a very woe;
Before, a joy proposed; behind, a dream.
  All this the world well knows; yet none knows well
  To shun the heaven that leads men to this hell.

My mistress' eyes are nothing like the sun

My mistress' eyes are nothing like the sun;
Coral is far more red than her lips' red:
If snow be white, why then her breasts are dun;
If hairs be wires, black wires grow on her head.
I have seen roses damaskt, red and white,
But no such roses see I in her cheeks;
And in some perfumes is there more delight
Than in the breath that from my mistress reeks.
I love to hear her speak, yet well I know
That music hath a far more pleasing sound;
I grant I never saw a goddess go;
My mistress, when she walks, treads on the ground.
And yet, by heaven, I think my love as rare
As any she belied with false compare.

When my love swears that she is made of truth

When my love swears that she is made of truth,
I do believe her, though I know she lies,
That she might think me some untutor'd youth,
Unlearned in the world's false subtleties.
Thus vainly thinking that she thinks me young,
Although she knows my days are past the best,
Simply I credit her false-speaking tongue:
On both sides thus is simple truth suppressed.
But wherefore says she not she is unjust?
And wherefore say not I that I am old?
O, love's best habit is in seeming trust,
And age in love loves not t' have years told:
Therefore I lie with her and she with me,
And in our faults by lies we flatter'd be.

Two loves I have of comfort and despair

Two loves I have of comfort and despair,
Which like two spirits do suggest me still:
The better angel is a man right fair,
The worser spirit a woman colour'd ill.
To win me soon to hell, my female evil
Tempteth my better angel from my side,
And would corrupt my saint to be a devil,
Wooing his purity with her foul pride.
And whether that my angel be turn'd fiend
Suspect I may, yet not directly tell;
But being both from me, both to each friend,
I guess one angel in another's hell:
  Yet this shall I ne'er know, but live in doubt,
  Till my bad angel fire my good one out.

Poor soul, the centre of my sinful earth

Poor soul, the centre of my sinful earth—
My sinful earth these rebel powers array—
Why dost thou pine within and suffer dearth,
Painting thy outward walls so costly gay?
Why so large cost, having so short a lease,
Dost thou upon thy fading mansion spend?
Shall worms, inheritors of this excess,
Eat up thy charge? is this thy body's end?
Then, soul, live thou upon thy servant's loss,
And let that pine to aggravate thy store;
Buy terms divine in selling hours of dross;
Within be fed, without be rich no more:
  So shalt thou feed on Death, that feeds on men,
  And Death once dead, there's no more dying then.

My love is as a fever, longing still

My love is as a fever, longing still
For that which longer nurseth the disease;
Feeding on that which doth preserve the ill,
Th' uncertain sickly appetite to please.
My reason, the physician to my love,
Angry that his prescriptions are not kept,
Hast left me, and I desperate now approve
Desire is death, which physic did except.
Past cure I am, now reason is past care,
And frantic-mad with evermore unrest;
My thoughts and my discourse as madmen's are,
At random from the truth vainly exprest;
For I have sworn thee fair, and thought thee bright,
Who art as black as hell, as dark as night.

JOHN DAVIES, OF HEREFORD

The author loving these homely meats specially, viz.: cream, pancakes, buttered pippin-pies (laugh, good people) and tobacco; writ to that worthy and virtuous gentlewoman, whom he calleth mistress, as followeth

If there were, oh! an Hellespont of cream
Between us, milk-white mistress, I would swim
To you, to show to both my love's extreme,
Leander-like,—yea! dive from brim to brim.
But met I with a buttered pippin-pie
Floating upon 't, that would I make my boat
To waft me to you without jeopardy,
Though sea-sick I might be while it did float.
Yet if a storm should rise, by night or day,
Of sugar-snows and hail of caraways,
Then, if I found a pancake in my way,
It like a plank should bring me to your kays;
Which having found, if they tobacco kept,
The smoke should dry me well before I slept.

The azured vault, the crystal circles bright

The azured vault, the crystal circles bright,
The gleaming fiery torches powdered there,
The changing round, the shining beamy light,
The sad and bearded fires, the monsters fair,
The prodigies appearing in the air,
The rearding[1] thunder, and the blustering winds,
The fowls in hue, in shape and nature rare,
The pretty notes that winged musicians finds,
In earth the savoury flowers, the metalled minds,[2]
The wholesome herbs, the haughty pleasant trees,
The silver streams, the beasts of sundry kinds,
The bounded roars and fishes of the seas;
All these for teaching man the Lord did frame,
To do His will whose glory shines in them.

SIR JOHN DAVIES

If you would know the love which I you bear

If you would know the love which I you bear,
Compare it to the Ring which your fair hand
Shall make more precious when you shall it wear:
So my love's nature you shall understand.
Is it of metal pure? so you shall prove
My love, which ne'er disloyal thought did stain.
Hath it no end? so endless is my love,
Unless you it destroy with your disdain.
Doth it the purer wax the more 'tis tried?
So doth my love: yet herein they dissent,
That whereas gold, the more 'tis purified,
By waxing less doth show some part is spent,
My love doth wax more pure by your more trying,
And yet increaseth in the purifying.

[1] roaring [2] mines

In this sweet book, the treasury of wit

In this sweet book, the treasury of wit,
All virtues, beauties, passions, written be:
And with such life they are set forth in it
As still methinks that which I read I see.
But this book's mistress is a living book
Which hath indeed those virtues in her mind,
And in whose face, though envy's self do look,
Even envy's eye shall all those beauties find.
Only the passions that are printed here
In her calm thoughts can no impression make:
She will not love, nor hate, nor hope, nor fear,
Though others seek these passions for her sake.
So in the sun, some say, there is no heat,
Though his reflecting beams do fire beget.

BEN JONSON

To the noble lady, the Lady Mary Wroth

I that have been a lover, and could shew it,
  Though not in these, in rithmes not wholly dumb,
  Since I exscribe your sonnets, am become
  A better lover, and much better poet.
Nor is my Muse or I ashamed to owe it
  To those true numerous graces; whereof some
  But charm the senses, others overcome
  Both brains and hearts; and mine now best do know it:
For in your verse all Cupid's armoury,
  His flames, his shafts, his quiver, and his bow,
  His very eyes are yours to overthrow.
But then his mother's sweets you so apply,
  Her joys, her smiles, her loves, as readers take
  For Venus' ceston every line you make.

As due by many titles I resign

As due by many titles I resign
My self to thee, O God; first, I was made
By thee, and for thee, and when I was decay'd
Thy blood bought that, the which before was thine;
I am thy son, made with thy self to shine,
Thy servant, whose pains thou hast still repaid,
Thy sheep, thine image, and, till I betray'd
My self, a temple of thy spirit divine;
Why doth the devil then usurp on me?
Why doth he steal, nay ravish that's my right?
Except thou rise and for thine own work fight,
Oh I shall soon despair, when I do see
That thou lov'st mankind well, yet wilt'not choose me,
And Satan hates me, yet is loth to lose me.

Oh my black soul! now art thou summoned

Oh my black soul! now art thou summoned
By sickness, death's herald, and champion;
Thou art like a pilgrim, which abroad hath done
Treason, and durst not turn to whence he is fled,
Or like a thief, which till death's doom be read,
Wisheth himself delivered from prison;
But damn'd and hal'd to execution,
Wisheth that still he might be imprisoned.
Yet grace, if thou repent, thou canst not lack;
But who shall give thee that grace to begin?
Oh make thy self with holy mourning black,
And red with blushing, as thou art with sin;
Or wash thee in Christ's blood, which hath this might—
That being red, it dyes red souls to white.

I am a little world made cunningly

I am a little world made cunningly
Of elements, and an angelic sprite,
But black sin hath betray'd to endless night
My world's both parts, and (oh!) both parts must die.
You which beyond that heaven which was most high
Have found new spheres, and of new lands can write,
Pour new seas in mine eyes, that so I might
Drown my world with my weeping earnestly,
Or wash it, if it must be drown'd no more:
But oh it must be burnt! alas the fire
Of lust and envy have burnt it heretofore,
And made it fouler. Let their flames retire,
And burn me, O Lord, with a fiery zeal
Of thee and thy house, which doth in eating heal.

At the round earth's imagin'd corners, blow

At the round earth's imagin'd corners, blow
Your trumpets, angels, and arise, arise
From death, you numberless infinities
Of souls, and to your scatter'd bodies go,
All whom the flood did, and fire shall o'erthrow,
All whom war, dearth, age, agues, tyrannies,
Despair, law, chance, hath slain, and you whose eyes
Shall behold God, and never taste death's woe.
But let them sleep, Lord, and me mourn a space,
For, if above all these, my sins abound,
'Tis late to ask abundance of thy grace,
When we are there. Here, on this lowly ground,
Teach me how to repent; for that's as good
As if thou hadst seal'd my pardon, with thy blood.

Death, be not proud, though some have called thee

Death, be not proud, though some have called thee
Mighty and dreadful, for thou art not so;
For those whom thou think'st thou dost overthrow
Die not, poor Death; nor yet canst thou kill me.
From rest and sleep, which but thy pictures be,
Much pleasure: then from thee much more must flow;
And soonest our best men with thee do go—
Rest of their bones and souls' delivery!
Thou'rt slave to fate, chance, kings and desperate men,
And dost with poison, war, and sickness dwell;
And poppy or charms can make us sleep as well,
And better than thy stroke. Why swell'st thou then?
One short sleep past, we wake eternally,
And death shall be no more: Death, thou shalt die.

What if this present were the world's last night

What if this present were the world's last night?
Mark in my heart, O soul, where thou dost dwell,
The picture of Christ crucified, and tell
Whether that countenance can thee affright,
Tears in his eyes quench the amazing light,
Blood fills his frowns, which from his pierc'd head fell.
And can that tongue adjudge thee unto hell,
Which pray'd forgiveness for his foes' fierce spite?
No, no; but as in my idolatry
I said to all my profane mistresses,
Beauty, of pity, foulness only is
A sign of rigour: so I say to thee,
To wicked spirits are horrid shapes assign'd,
This beauteous form assures a piteous mind.

Batter my heart, three-personed God

Batter my heart, three-personed God; for, you
As yet but knock, breathe, shine, and seek to mend;
That I may rise, and stand, o'erthrow me, and bend
Your force, to break, blow, burn and make me new.
I, like an usurpt town, to another due,
Labour to admit you, but Oh, to no end.
Reason, your viceroy in me, me should defend,
But is captiv'd, and proves weak or untrue.
Yet dearly I love you, and would be loved fain,
But am betrothed unto your enemy:
Divorce me, untie or break that knot again,
Take me to you, imprison me, for I
Except you enthrall me, never shall be free,
Nor ever chaste, except you ravish me.

Since she whom I lov'd hath paid her last debt

Since she whom I lov'd hath paid her last debt
To nature, and to hers, and my good is dead,
And her soul early into heaven ravished,
Wholly on heavenly things my mind is set.
Here the admiring her my mind did whet
To seek thee, God; so streams do show their head;
But though I have found thee, and thou my thirst hath fed,
A holy thirsty dropsy melts me yet.
But why should I beg more love, when as thou
Dost woo my soul for hers, offering all thine,
And dost not only fear lest I allow
My love to saints and angels, things divine,
But in thy tender jealousy dost doubt
Lest the world, flesh, yea devil put thee out.

Show me, dear Christ, thy spouse, so bright and clear

Show me, dear Christ, thy spouse, so bright and clear.
What! is it She, which on the other shore
Goes richly painted? or which rob'd and tore
Laments and mourns in Germany and here?
Sleeps she a thousand, then peeps up one year?
Is she self truth, and errs? now new, now outwore?
Doth she, and did she, and shall she evermore
On one, on seven, or on no hill appear?
Dwells she with us, or like adventuring knights
First travaile we to seek and then make love?
Betray, kind husband, thy spouse to our sights,
And let mine amorous soul court thy mild dove,
Who is most true, and pleasing to thee, then
When she's embrac'd and open to most men.

Oh, to vex me, contraries meet in one

Oh, to vex me, contraries meet in one:
Inconstancy unnaturally hath begot
A constant habit; that when I would not
I change in vows, and in devotion.
As humorous is my contrition
As my profane love, and as soon forgot;
As riddlingly distemper'd, cold and hot,
As praying, as mute; as infinite, as none.
I durst not view heaven yesterday; and today
In prayers, and flattering speeches I court God:
Tomorrow I quake with true fear of his rod.
So my devout fits come and go away
Like a fantastic ague; save that here
Those are my best days, when I shake with fear.

RICHARD BARNFIELD

If Music and sweet Poetry agree

If Music and sweet Poetry agree,
As they must needs, (the sister and the brother),
Then must the love be great 'twixt thee and me,
Because thou lovest the one and I the other.
Dowland to thee is dear, whose heavenly touch
Upon the lute doth ravish human sense;
Spenser to me, whose deep conceit is such
As, passing all conceit, needs no defence.
Thou lovest to hear the sweet melodious sound
That Phoebus' lute, the Queen of Music, makes;
And I in deep delight am chiefly drowned
Whenas himself to singing he betakes.
One god is god of both, as poets feign;
One knight loves both, and both in thee remain.

LORD HERBERT OF CHERBURY

Black Itself

Thou black, wherein all colours are composed,
And unto which they all at last return,
Thou colour of the sun where it doth burn,
And shadow, where it cools, in thee is closed
Whatever nature can or hath disposed
In any other hue: from thee do rise
Those tempers and complexions, which, disclosed
As parts of thee, do work as mysteries
Of that thy hidden power: when thou dost reign,
The characters of fate shine in the skies,
And tell us what the heavens do ordain,
But when earth's common light shines to our eyes,
Thou so retirest thyself, that thy disdain
All revelation unto man denies.

Lord, thus I sin, repent, and sin again

Lord, thus I sin, repent, and sin again,
As if repentance only were in me
Leave for new sin; thus do I entertain
My short time and thy grace abusing thee
And thy long-suffering, which, though it be
Ne'er overcome by sin, yet were in vain
If tempted oft: thus we our errors see
Before our punishment, and so remain
Without excuse; and, Lord, in them 'tis true
Thy laws are just; but why dost thou distrain
Aught else for life save life? That is thy due,
The rest thou mak'st us owe, and mayst to us
As well forgive—but oh! my sins renew,
Whilst I do talk with my Creator thus.

WILLIAM DRUMMOND OF HAWTHORNDEN

I know that all beneath the moon decays

I know that all beneath the moon decays,
And what by mortals in this world is brought,
In Time's great periods shall return to nought;
That fairest states have fatal nights and days;
I know how all the Muse's heavenly lays,
With toil of spright which are so dearly bought,
As idle sounds of few or none are sought,
And that nought lighter is than airy praise.
I know frail beauty like the purple flower,
To which one morn oft birth and death affords;
That love a jarring is of minds' accords,
Where sense and will invassal reason's power:
Know what I list, this all can not me move,
But that, O me! I both must write and love.

Sleep, Silence' child, sweet father of soft rest

Sleep, Silence' child, sweet father of soft rest,
Prince whose approach peace to all mortals brings,
Indifferent host to shepherds and to kings,
Sole comforter of minds with grief opprest;
Lo, by thy charming-rod all breathing things
Lie slumbering, with forgetfulness possest,
And yet o'er me to spread thy drowsy wings
Thou spares, alas! who cannot be thy guest.
Since I am thine, O come, but with that face
To inward light which thou art wont to show;
With feigned solace each a true-felt woe;
Or if, deaf god, thou do deny that grace,
Come as thou wilt, and what thou wilt bequeath,—
I long to kiss the image of my death.

No trust in Time

Look how the flower which lingeringly doth fade,
The morning's darling late, the summer's queen,
Spoiled of that juice which kept it fresh and green,
As high as it did raise, bows low the head:
Right so my life, contentments being dead,
Or in their contraries but only seen,
With swifter speed declines than erst it spread,
And blasted, scarce now shows what it hath been.
As doth the pilgrim therefore, whom the night
By darkness would imprison on his way,
Think on thy home, my soul, and think aright
Of what yet rests thee of life's wasting day;
Thy sun posts westward, passed is thy morn,
And twice it is not given thee to be born.

The Book of the World

Of this fair volume which we World do name
If we the sheets and leaves could turn with care,
Of him who it corrects and did it frame,
We clear might read the art and wisdom rare:
Find out his power which wildest powers doth tame,
His providence existing everywhere,
His justice which proud rebels doth not spare,
In every page, no, period of the same.
But silly we, like foolish children, rest
Well pleased with coloured vellum, leaves of gold,
Fair dangling ribands, leaving what is best,
On the great writer's sense ne'er taking hold;
Or if by chance our minds do muse on ought,
It is some picture on the margin wrought.

St John the Baptist

The last and greatest herald of Heaven's King,
Girt with rough skins, hies to the deserts wild,
Among that savage brood the woods forth bring,
Which he than man more harmless found and mild.
His food was blossoms, and what young did spring,
With honey that from virgin hives distilled;
Parched body, hollow eyes, some uncouth thing
Made him appear, long since from earth exiled.
There burst he forth: All ye whose hopes rely
On God, with me amidst these deserts mourn,
Repent, repent, and from old errors turn!—
Who listened to his voice, obeyed his cry?
Only the echoes, which he made relent,
Rung from their marble caves, Repent! Repent!

Fairest, when by the rules of palmistry

Fairest, when by the rules of palmistry
You took my hand to try if you could guess,
By lines therein, if any wight there be
Ordained to make me know some happiness,
I wished that those characters could explain
Whom I will never wrong with hope to win;
Or that by them a copy might be seen
By you, O Love, what thoughts I have within.
But since the hand of Nature did not set
(As providently loth to have it known)
The means to find that hidden alphabet,
Mine eyes shall be th' interpreters alone.
By them conceive my thoughts and tell me, fair,
If now you see her that doth love me there!

Lo, I am the man that whilom loved and lost

Lo, I am the man that whilom loved and lost,
  Not dreading loss, do sing again of love;
  And like a man but lately tempest-tost
  Try if my stars still inauspicious prove;
Not to make good that poets never can
  Long time without a chosen mistress be,
  Do I sing thus; or my affections ran
  Within the maze of mutability;
What last I loved was beauty of the mind,
  And that lodged in a temple truly fair,
  Which ruined now by death, if I can find
  The Saint that lived therein some otherwhere,
I may adore it there, and love the cell
  For entertaining what I loved so well.

To his mistress, objecting to him neither toying nor talking

You say I love not, 'cause I do not play
Still with your curls, and kiss the time away.
You blame me, too, because I can't devise
Some sport to please those babies in your eyes;—
By Love's religion, I must here confess it,
The most I love, when I the least express it.
Small griefs find tongues; full casks are ever found
To give, if any, yet but little sound.
Deep waters noiseless are; and this we know,
That chiding streams betray small depth below.
So when love speechless is, she doth express
A depth in love, and that depth bottomless.
Now, since my love is tongueless, know me such,
Who speak but little, 'cause I love so much.

GEORGE HERBERT

The Sinner

Lord, how I am all ague, when I seek
What I have treasured in my memory!
Since, if my soul make even with the week,
Each seventh note by right is due to thee.

I find there quarries of piled vanities,
But shreds of holiness, that dare not venture
To show their face, since cross to thy decrees:
There the circumference earth is, heaven the centre.

In so much dregs the quintessence is small:
The spirit and good extract of my heart
Comes to about the many hundredth part.
Yet, Lord, restore thine image, hear my call:

And thou my hard heart scarce to thee can groan,
Remember that thou once didst write in stone.

Redemption

Having been tenant long to a rich Lord,
  Not thriving, I resolved to be bold,
  And make a suit unto him, to afford
A new small-rented lease, and cancel th' old.

In Heaven at his manor I him sought:
  They told me there, that he was lately gone
  About some land, which he had dearly bought
Long since on earth, to take possession.

I straight return'd, and knowing his great birth,
  Sought him accordingly in great resorts;
  In cities, theatres, gardens, parks, and courts:
At length I heard a ragged noise and mirth

  Of thieves and murderers: there I him espied,
  Who straight, *Your suit is granted*, said, and died.

Prayer

Prayer, the Church's banquet, Angel's age,
  God's breath in man returning to his birth,
  The soul in paraphrase, heart in pilgrimage,
The Christian plummet sounding heaven and earth;

Engine against th' Almighty, sinner's tower,
  Reversed thunder, Christ-side-piercing spear,
  The six days' world-transposing in an hour,
A kind of tune, which all things hear and fear;

Softness, and peace, and joy, and love, and bliss,
  Exalted Manna, gladness of the best,
  Heaven in ordinary, men well drest,
The Milky Way, the bird of Paradise,

  Church-bells beyond the stars heard, the soul's blood,
  The land of spices, something understood.

The Son

Let foreign nations of their language boast,
What fine variety each tongue affords:
I like our language, as our men and coast;
Who cannot dress it well, want wit, not words.
How neatly do we give one only name
To Parent's issue and the Sun's bright star!
A Son is light and fruit; a fruitful flame
Chasing the Father's dimness, carried far
From the first man in the East, to fresh and new
Western discoveries of posterity.
So in one word our Lord's humility
We turn upon him in a sense most true:
　For what Christ once in humbleness began,
　We him in glory call, *The Son of Man.*

The Answer

My comforts drop and melt away like snow:
I shake my head, and all the thoughts and ends,
Which my fierce youth did bandy, fall and flow
Like leaves about me, or like summer friends,
Flies of estates and sunshine. But to all,
Who think me eager, hot, and undertaking,
But in my prosecutions slack and small;
As a young exhalation, newly waking,
Scorns his first bed of dirt, and means the sky;
But cooling by the way, grows pursy and slow,
And settling to a cloud, doth live and die
In that dark state of tears: to all, that so
Show me, and set me, I have one reply,
Which they that know the rest, know more than I.

A sonnet,[1] *sent by George Herbert to his mother as a New Year's gift from Cambridge*

My God, where is that ancient heat towards thee,
  Wherewith whole shoals of Martyrs once did burn,
Besides their other flames? Doth poetry
  Wear Venus' livery? only serve her turn?
Why are not sonnets made of thee? and lays
  Upon thine altar burnt? Cannot thy love
Heighten a spirit to sound out thy praise
  As well as any she? Cannot thy Dove
Outstrip their Cupid easily in flight?
  Or, since thy ways are deep, and still the same,
  Will not a verse run smooth that bears thy name?
Why doth that fire, which by thy power and might
  Each breast does feel, no braver fuel choose
  Than that which, one day, worms may chance refuse?
Sure, Lord, there is enough in thee to dry
  Oceans of ink; for, as the Deluge did
Cover the earth, so doth thy Majesty:
  Each cloud distils thy praise, and doth forbid
Poets to turn it to another use.
  Roses and lilies speak thee; and to make
A pair of cheeks of them, is thy abuse.
  Why should I women's eyes for crystal take?
Such poor invention burns in their low mind
  Whose fire is wild, and doth not upward go
  To praise, and on thee, Lord, some ink bestow.
Open the bones, and you shall nothing find
  In the best face but filth; when, Lord, in thee
  The beauty lies, in the discovery.

[1] In fact, two sonnets

A Rose

Blown in the morning, thou shalt fade ere noon.
What boots a life which in such haste forsakes thee?
Thou'rt wondrous frolic, being to die so soon,
And passing proud a little colour makes thee.
If thee thy brittle beauty so deceives,
Know then the thing that swells thee is thy bane;
For the same beauty doth, in bloody leaves,
The sentence of thy early death contain.
Some clown's coarse lungs will poison thy sweet flower,
If by the careless plough thou shalt be torn;
And many Herods lie in wait each hour
To murder thee as soon as thou art born—
  Nay, force thy bud to blow—their tyrant breath
  Anticipating life, to hasten death!

JOHN MILTON

How soon hath Time, the subtle thief of youth

How soon hath Time, the subtle thief of youth,
  Stol'n on his wing my three and twentieth year!
  My hasting days fly on with full career,
  But my late spring no bud or blossom shew'th.
Perhaps my semblance might deceive the truth,
  That I to manhood am arriv'd so near,
  And inward ripeness doth much less appear,
  That some more timely-happy spirits indueth.
Yet be it less or more, or soon or slow,
  It shall be still in strictest measure even
  To that same lot, however mean, or high,
Toward which Time leads me, and the will of Heaven;
  All is, if I have grace to use it so,
  As ever in my great task-Master's eye.

To the Nightingale

O Nightingale! that on yon bloomy spray
  Warblest at eve, when all the woods are still,
  Thou with fresh hope the lover's heart dost fill,
While the jolly hours lead on propitious May.
Thy liquid notes that close the eye of day,
  First heard before the shallow cuckoo's bill,
  Portend success in love. O, if Jove's will
Have linked that amorous power to thy soft lay,
Now timely sing, ere the rude bird of hate
  Foretell my hopeless doom, in some grove nigh;
As thou from year to year hast sung too late
  For my relief, yet hadst no reason why.
Whether the Muse or Love call thee his mate,
  Both them I serve, and of their train am I.

When the Assault was Intended to the City

Captain or Colonel, or Knight in Arms,
  Whose chance on these defenceless doors may seize,
  If deed of honour did thee ever please,
Guard them, and him within protect from harms.
He can requite thee; for he knows the charms
  That call fame on such gentle acts as these,
  And he can spread thy name o'er lands and seas,
Whatever clime the sun's bright circle warms.
Lift not thy spear against the Muses' bower!
  The great Emathian conqueror bid spare
The house of Pindarus, when temple and tower
  Went to the ground; and the repeated air
Of sad Electra's poet had the power
  To save the Athenian walls from ruin bare.

To the Lady Margaret Ley

Daughter of that good Earl, once President
  Of England's Council and her Treasury,
  Who lived in both unstained with gold or fee,
And left them both, more in himself content,
Till the sad breaking of that Parliament
  Broke him, as that dishonest victory
  At Chaeronea, fatal to liberty,
Killed with report that old man eloquent:
Though later born than to have known the days
  Wherein your father flourished, yet by you,
    Madam, methinks I see him living yet:
So well your words his noble virtues praise
  That all both judge you to relate them true
    And to possess them, honoured Margaret.

To Mr. H. Lawes on His Airs

Harry, whose tuneful and well-measured song
  First taught our English music how to span
  Words with just note and accent, not to scan
With Midas' ears, committing short and long,
Thy worth and skill exempts thee from the throng,
  With praise enough for Envy to look wan;
  To after age thou shalt be writ the man
That with smooth air couldst humour best our tongue.
Thou honour'st Verse, and Verse must send her wing
  To honour thee, the priest of Phoebus' quire,
    That tunest their happiest lines in hymn or story.
  Dante shall give Fame leave to set thee higher
Than his Casella, whom he wooed to sing,
    Met in the milder shades of Purgatory.

To the Lord General Cromwell, May 1652, on the Proposals of Certain Ministers at the Committee for Propagation of the Gospel

Cromwell, our chief of men, who through a cloud
  Not of war only, but detractions rude,
  Guided by faith and matchless fortitude,
To peace and truth thy glorious way hast ploughed,
And on the neck of crowned Fortune proud
  Hast reared God's trophies, and His work pursued,
  While Darwen stream, with blood of Scots imbrued,
And Dunbar field, resounds thy praises loud,
And Worcester's laureate wreath: yet much remains
  To conquer still; Peace hath her victories
  No less renowned than War: new foes arise,
Threatening to bind our souls with secular chains.
    Help us to save free conscience from the paw
    Of hireling wolves, whose Gospel is their maw.

To Sir Henry Vane the Younger

Vane, young in years, but in sage counsel old,
  Than whom a better senator ne'er held
  The helm of Rome, when gowns, not arms, repelled
The fierce Epirot and the African bold,
Whether to settle peace, or to unfold
  The drift of hollow states hard to be spelled;
  Then to advise how war may, best upheld,
Move by her two main nerves, iron and gold,
In all her equipage; besides, to know
  Both spiritual power and civil, what each means,
    What severs each, thou hast learned, which few have done.
The bounds of either sword to thee we owe:
  Therefore on thy firm hand Religion leans
    In peace, and reckons thee her eldest son.

On the Lord General Fairfax, at the siege of Colchester

Fairfax, whose name in arms through Europe rings,
Filling each mouth with envy or with praise,
And all her jealous monarchs with amaze,
And rumours loud that daunt remotest kings,
Thy firm unshaken virtue ever brings
Victory home, though new rebellions raise
Their Hydra-heads, and the false North displays
Her broken league to imp their serpent wings.
O yet a nobler task awaits thy hand!
For what can war but endless war still breed,
Till truth and right from violence be freed,
And public faith cleared from the shameful brand
Of public fraud? In vain doth Valour bleed
While Avarice and Rapine share the land.

On the Detraction which Followed Upon My Writing Certain Treatises

A book was writ of late called *Tetrachordon*,
And woven close, both matter, form and style;
The subject new, it walked the town a while,
Numbering good intellects: now seldom pored on.
Cries the stall-reader, 'Bless us! what a word on
A title-page is this!'; and some in file
Stand spelling false, while one might walk to Mile-
End Green. Why is it harder, sirs, than *Gordon*,
Colkitto, or *Macdonnel*, or *Galasp*?
Those rugged names to our like mouths grow sleek,
That would have made Quintalian stare and gasp.
Thy age, like ours, O soul of Sir John Cheek,
Hated not learning worse than toad or asp,
When thou taught'st Cambridge and King Edward Greek.

On the Late Massacre in Piedmont

Avenge, O Lord, thy slaughtered saints, whose bones
Lie scattered on the Alpine mountains cold;
  Even them who kept thy truth so pure of old,
When all our Fathers worshipped stocks and stones,
Forget not: in thy book record their groans
  Who were thy sheep, and in their ancient fold
  Slain by the bloody Piedmontese, that rolled
Mother with infant down the rocks. Their moans
The vales redoubled to the hills, and they
  To heaven. Their martyred blood and ashes sow
O'er all the Italian fields, where still doth sway
  The triple Tyrant; that from these may grow
A hundredfold, who, having learnt thy way,
  Early may fly the Babylonian woe.

On his Blindness

When I consider how my light is spent,
  Ere half my days in this dark world and wide,
  And that one talent which is death to hide
Lodged with me useless, though my soul more bent
To serve therewith my Maker, and present
  My true account, lest he, returning, chide,
  'Doth God exact day-labour, light denied?'
I fondly ask. But Patience, to prevent
That murmur, soon replies, 'God doth not need
  Either man's work or his own gifts. Who best
    Bear his mild yoke, they serve him best. His State
Is kingly. Thousands at his bidding speed,
  And post o'er land and ocean without rest;
    They also serve who only stand and wait.'

To Mr. Lawrence

Lawrence, of virtuous father virtuous son,
Now that the fields are dank, and ways are mire,
Where shall we sometimes meet, and by the fire
Help waste a sullen day, what may be won
From the hard season gaining? Time will run
On smoother, till Favonius reinspire
The frozen earth, and clothe in fresh attire
The lily and rose, that neither sowed nor spun.
What neat repast shall feast us, light and choice,
Of Attic taste, with wine, whence we may rise
To hear the lute well touched, or artful voice
Warble immortal notes and Tuscan air?
He who of those delights can judge, and spare
To interpose them oft, is not unwise.

To Cyriack Skinner

Cyriack, whose grandsire on the royal bench
Of British Themis, with no mean applause,
Pronounced, and in his volumes taught, our Laws,
Which others at their Bar so often wrench,
To-day deep thoughts resolve with me to drench
In mirth, that after no repenting draws;
Let Euclid rest, and Archimedes pause,
And what the Swede intend, and what the French.
To measure life learn thou betimes, and know
Toward solid good what leads the nearest way;
For other things mild Heaven a time ordains,
And disapproves that care, though wise in show,
That with superfluous burden loads the day,
And, when God sends a cheerful hour, refrains.

To the Same upon his Blindness

Cyriack, this three years' day these eyes, though clear,
  To outward view, of blemish or of spot,
  Bereft of light, their seeing have forgot;
Nor to their idle orbs doth sight appear
Of sun, or moon, or star, throughout the year,
  Or man, or woman. Yet I argue not
  Against Heaven's hand or will, nor bate a jot
Of heart or hope; but still bear up and steer
Right onward. What supports me, dost thou ask?
  The conscience, friend, to have lost them overplied
In Liberty's defence, my noble task,
  Of which all Europe rings from side to side.
This thought might lead me through the world's vain mask
  Content, though blind, had I no better guide.

On his Deceased Wife

Methought I saw my late espoused Saint
  Brought to me like Alcestis from the grave,
  Whom Jove's great son to her glad husband gave,
  Rescued from death by force, though pale and faint.
Mine, as whom washt from spot of child-bed taint
  Purification in the old Law did save,
  And such, as yet once more I trust to have
  Full sight of her in Heaven without restraint,
Came vested all in white, pure as her mind.
  Her face was veiled; yet to my fancied sight
  Love, sweetness, goodness, in her person shined
So clear, as in no face with more delight.
  But O as to embrace me she inclined,
  I waked, she fled, and day brought back my night.

On the Death of Richard West

In vain to me the smiling mornings shine,
  And reddening Phoebus lifts his golden fire;
The birds in vain their amorous descant join,
  Or cheerful fields resume their green attire:
These ears, alas! for other notes repine,
  A different object do these eyes require;
My lonely anguish melts no heart but mine,
  And in my breast the imperfect joys expire.
Yet morning smiles the busy race to cheer,
  And new-born pleasure brings to happier men;
The fields to all their wonted tribute bear,
  To warm their little loves the birds complain:
I fruitless mourn to him that cannot hear,
  And weep the more because I weep in vain.

THOMAS WARTON

When late the trees were stript by Winter pale

When late the trees were stript by Winter pale,
  Young Health, a dryad-maid in vesture green,
  Or like the forest's silver-quiver'd queen,
On airy uplands met the piercing gale;
And, ere its earliest echo shook the vale,
  Watching the hunter's joyous horn was seen.
  But since, gay-thron'd in fiery chariot sheen,
Summer has smote each daisy-dappled dale,
She to the cave retires, high-arched beneath
  The fount that laves proud Isis' towery brim;
And now all glad the temperate air to breathe,
  While cooling drops distil from arches dim,
Binding her dewy locks with sedgy wreath
  She sits amid the quire of Naiads trim.

THOMAS WARTON

To the River Lodon

Ah! what a weary race my feet have run
Since first I trod thy banks with alders crowned,
And thought my way was all through fairy ground,
Beneath thy azure sky and golden sun,
Where first my Muse to lisp her notes begun.
While pensive Memory traces back the round
Which fills the varied interval between,
Much pleasure, more of sorrow, marks the scene.
Sweet native stream, those skies and suns so pure
No more return to cheer my evening road,
Yet still one joy remains, that not obscure
Nor useless all my vacant days have flowed
From Youth's grey dawn to manhood's prime mature,
Nor with the Muse's laurel unbestowed.

WILLIAM COWPER

To Mrs. Unwin

Mary! I want a lyre with other strings,
  Such aid from heaven as some have feigned they drew,
  An eloquence scarce given to mortals, new
And undebased by praise of meaner things;
That, ere through age or woe I shed my wings,
  I may record thy worth with honour due,
  In verse as musical as thou art true,
And that immortalizes whom it sings.
But thou hast little need. There is a Book
  By seraphs writ with beams of heavenly light,
On which the eyes of God not rarely look,
  A chronicle of actions just and bright;—
    There all thy deeds, my faithful Mary, shine;
    And since thou own'st that praise, I spare thee mine.

Composed upon Westminster Bridge September 3rd, 1802

Earth has not anything to show more fair:
  Dull would he be of soul who could pass by
  A sight so touching in its majesty:
This City now doth, like a garment, wear
The beauty of the morning; silent, bare,
  Ships, towers, domes, theatres, and temples lie
  Open unto the fields, and to the sky;
All bright and glittering in the smokeless air.
Never did sun more beautifully steep
  In his first splendour, valley, rock, or hill;
Ne'er saw I, never felt, a calm so deep!
  The river glideth at his own sweet will:
Dear God! the very houses seem asleep;
  And all that mighty heart is lying still!

On the Extinction of the Venetian Republic

Once did She hold the gorgeous East in fee;
  And was the safeguard of the West: the worth
  Of Venice did not fall below her birth,
Venice, the eldest Child of Liberty.
She was a maiden City, bright and free:
  No guile seduced, no force could violate;
  And when she took unto herself a Mate,
She must espouse the everlasting Sea.
And what if she had seen those glories fade,
  Those titles vanish, and that strength decay?
Yet shall some tribute of regret be paid
  When her long life had reached its final day;
Men are we, and must grieve when even the Shade
  Of that which once was great is passed away.

London 1802

i

Milton! thou shouldst be living at this hour;
England hath need of thee; she is a fen
Of stagnant waters; altar, sword, and pen,
Fireside, the heroic wealth of hall and bower,
Have forfeited their ancient English dower
Of inward happiness. We are selfish men;
Oh! raise us up, return to us again;
And give us manners, virtue, freedom, power.
Thy soul was like a Star, and dwelt apart:
Thou hadst a voice whose sound was like the sea;
Pure as the naked heavens, majestic, free,
So didst thou travel on life's common way,
In cheerful godliness; and yet thy heart
The lowliest duties on herself did lay.

ii

Great men have been among us; hands that penned
And tongues that uttered wisdom—better none:
The later Sidney, Marvell, Harrington,
Young Vane, and others who called Milton friend.
These moralists could act and comprehend:
They knew how genuine glory was put on;
Taught us how rightfully a nation shone
In splendour: what strength was that would not bend
But in magnanimous meekness. France, 'tis strange,
Hath brought forth no such souls as we had then.
Perpetual emptiness! unceasing change!
No single volume paramount, no code,
No master spirit, no determined road;
But equally a want of books and men!

iii

It is not to be thought of that the Flood
Of British freedom, which, to the open sea
Of the world's praise, from dark antiquity
Hath flowed, 'with pomp of waters, unwithstood,'
Roused though it be full often to a mood
Which spurns the cheek of salutary bands,—
That this most famous Stream in bogs and sands
Should perish; and to evil and to good
Be lost for ever. In our halls is hung
Armoury of the invincible Knights of old:
We must be free or die, who speak the tongue
That Shakespeare spake; the faith and morals hold
Which Milton held.—In every thing we are sprung
Of Earth's first blood, have titles manifold.

iv

When I have borne in memory what has tamed
Great nations, how ennobling thoughts depart
When men change swords for ledgers, and desert
The student's bower for gold, some fears unnamed
I had, my country!—am I to be blamed?
But when I think of thee, and what thou art,
Verily, in the bottom of my heart,
Of those unfilial fears I am ashamed.
But dearly must we prize thee; we who find
In thee a bulwark for the cause of men;
And I by my affection was beguiled.
What wonder if a poet now and then,
Among the many movements of his mind,
Felt for thee as a lover or a child?

To Toussaint l'Ouverture

Toussaint, the most unhappy man of men!
Whether the whistling Rustic tend his plough
Within thy hearing, or thy head be now
Pillowed in some deep dungeon's earless den;—
O miserable Chieftain! where and when
Wilt thou find patience? Yet die not; do thou
Wear rather in thy bonds a cheerful brow:
Though fallen thyself, never to rise again,
Live, and take comfort. Thou hast left behind
Powers that will work for thee; air, earth, and skies;
There's not a breathing of the common wind
That will forget thee; thou hast great allies;
Thy friends are exultations, agonies,
And love, and man's unconquerable mind.

The world is too much with us

The world is too much with us; late and soon,
Getting and spending, we lay waste our powers:
Little we see in Nature that is ours;
We have given our hearts away, a sordid boon!
This Sea that bares her bosom to the moon;
The winds that will be howling at all hours,
And are up-gathered now like sleeping flowers;
For this, for every thing, we are out of tune;
It moves us not.—Great God! I'd rather be
A Pagan suckled in a creed outworn;
So might I, standing on this pleasant lea,
Have glimpses that would make me less forlorn;
Have sight of Proteus rising from the sea;
Or hear old Triton blow his wreathed horn.

After-thought (River Duddon)

I thought of Thee, my partner and my guide,
  As being past away.—Vain sympathies!
  For, backward, Duddon, as I cast my eyes,
I see what was, and is, and will abide;
Still glides the Stream, and shall for ever glide;
  The Form remains, the Function never dies;
  While we, the brave, the mighty, and the wise,
We Men, who in our morn of youth defied
The elements, must vanish; be it so!
  Enough, if something from our hands have power
  To live, and act, and serve the future hour;
And if, as toward the silent tomb we go,
  Through love, through hope, and faith's transcendent dower,
We feel that we are greater than we know.

Surprised by joy

Surprised by joy—impatient as the Wind
  I turned to share the transport—Oh! with whom
  But Thee, deep buried in the silent tomb,
That spot which no vicissitude can find?
Love, faithful love, recalled thee to my mind—
  But how could I forget thee?—Through what power,
  Even for the least division of an hour,
Have I been so beguiled as to be blind
To my most grievous loss!—That thought's return
  Was the worst pang that sorrow ever bore,
Save one, one only, when I stood forlorn,
  Knowing my heart's best treasure was no more;
That neither present time, nor years unborn,
  Could to my sight that heavenly face restore.

Scorn not the Sonnet

Scorn not the Sonnet; Critic, you have frowned,
Mindless of its just honours: with this key
Shakespeare unlocked his heart; the melody
Of this small lute gave ease to Petrarch's wound;
A thousand times this pipe did Tasso sound;
With it Camoens soothed an exile's grief;
The Sonnet glittered a gay myrtle leaf
Amid the cypress with which Dante crowned
His visionary brow; a glow-worm lamp
It cheered mild Spenser, called from Faery-land
To struggle through dark ways; and when a damp
Fell round the path of Milton, in his hand
The Thing became a trumpet, whence he blew
Soul-animating strains—alas, too few!

At Sunset

It is a beauteous Evening, calm and free,
  The holy time is quiet as a Nun
  Breathless with adoration; the broad sun
Is sinking down in its tranquillity;
The gentleness of heaven broods o'er the sea;
  Listen! the mighty Being is awake,
  And doth with his eternal motion make
A sound like thunder—everlastingly.
Dear Child! dear Girl! that walkest with me here,
  If thou appear untouched by solemn thought,
    Thy nature is not therefore less divine;
Thou liest in Abraham's bosom all the year;
    And worship'st at the Temple's inner shrine,
  God being with thee when we know it not.

Two Ships

i

With ships the sea was sprinkled far and nigh,
  Like stars in heaven, and joyously it showed;
  Some lying fast at anchor in the road,
Some veering up and down, one knew not why.
A goodly vessel did I then espy
  Come like a giant from a haven broad;
  And lustily along the bay she strode,
Her tackling rich, and of apparel high.
This ship was nought to me, nor I to her,
  Yet I pursued her with a Lover's look;
This ship to all the rest did I prefer:
  When will she turn, and whither? She will brook
No tarrying; where She comes the winds must stir:
  On went She,—and due north her journey took.

ii

Where lies the land to which yon ship must go?
  Fresh as a lark mounting at break of day
  Festively she puts forth in trim array;
Is she for tropic suns, or polar snow?
What boots the inquiry?—Neither friend nor foe
  She cares for; let her travel where she may,
  She finds familiar names, a beaten way
Ever before her, and a wind to blow.
Yet still I ask, what haven is her mark?
  And, almost as it was when ships were rare,
  (From time to time, like pilgrims, here and there
Crossing the waters) doubt, and something dark,
  Of the old sea some reverential fear,
Is with me at thy farewell, joyous bark!

Thought of a Briton on the Subjugation of Switzerland

Two Voices are there; one is of the Sea,
  One of the Mountains; each a mighty Voice:
  In both from age to age thou didst rejoice,
They were thy chosen music, Liberty!
There came a Tyrant, and with holy glee
  Thou foughtst against him; but hast vainly striven:
  Thou from thy Alpine holds at length art driven,
Where not a torrent murmurs heard by thee.
Of one deep bliss thine ear hath been bereft:
Then cleave, O cleave to that which still is left;
  For, high-souled Maid, what sorrow would it be
That Mountain floods should thunder as before,
And Ocean bellow from his rocky shore,
  And neither awful Voice be heard by thee!

SAMUEL TAYLOR COLERIDGE

On Receiving a Letter Informing Me of the Birth of a Son

When they did greet me father, sudden awe
Weighed down my spirit: I retired and knelt,
Seeking the throne of grace, but inly felt
No heavenly visitation upwards draw
My feeble mind, nor cheering ray impart.
Ah me! before the Eternal Sire I brought
The unquiet silence of confused thought
And shapeless feelings: my o'erwhelmed heart
Trembled, and vacant tears streamed down my face.
And now once more, O Lord, to thee I bend,
Lover of souls, and groan for future grace,
That ere my babe youth's perilous maze have trod
Thy overshadowing Spirit may descend,
And he be born again, a child of God.

To Nature

It may indeed be phantasy when I
Essay to draw from all created things
Deep, heartfelt, inward joy that closely clings;
And trace in leaves and flowers that round me lie
Lessons of love and earnest piety.
So let it be; and if the wide world rings
In mock of this belief, to me it brings
Nor fear, nor grief, nor vain perplexity.
So will I build my altar in the fields,
And the blue sky my fretted dome shall be,
And the sweet fragrance that the wild flower yields
Shall be the incense I will yield to Thee,
Thee only God! and Thou shalt not despise
Even me, the priest of this poor sacrifice.

To Richard Brinsley Sheridan, Esq.

It was some spirit, Sheridan, that breathed
O'er thy young mind such wildly various power!
My soul hath marked thee in her shaping hour,
Thy temples with Hymettian flowerets wreathed:
And sweet thy voice as when o'er Laura's bier
Sad music trembled through Valclusa's glade,
Sweet as at dawn the love-lorn serenade
That wafts soft dreams to Slumber's listening ear.
Now patriot Rage and Indignation high
Swell the full tones! And now thine eye-beams dance
Meanings of scorn and wit's quaint revelry.
Writhes inly from the bosom-piercing glance
The Apostate by the brainless rout adored
As erst that elder fiend beneath great Michael's sword.

Fancy in Nubibus: or the Poet in the Clouds

O it is pleasant, with a heart at ease,
Just after sunset, or by moonlight skies,
To make the shifting clouds be what you please,
Or let the easily-persuaded eyes
Own each quaint likeness issuing from the mould
Of a friend's fancy; or, with head bent low
And cheek aslant, see rivers flow of gold
'Twixt crimson banks; and then, a traveller, go
From mount to mount through Cloudland, gorgeous land!
Or listening to the tide, with closed sight,
Be that blind bard who, on the Chian strand
By those deep sounds possessed with inward light,
Beheld the Iliad and the Odyssee
Rise to the swelling of the voiceful sea.

To the River Otter

Dear native brook! wild streamlet of the West!
How many various-fated years have passed,
What happy, and what mournful hours, since last
I skimmed the smooth thin stone along thy breast,
Numbering its light leaps! Yet so deep imprest
Sink the sweet scenes of childhood, that mine eyes
I never shut amid the sunny ray,
But straight with all their tints thy waters rise,
Thy crossing plank, thy marge with willows gray,
And bedded sand that, veined with various dyes,
Gleamed through thy bright transparence. On my way,
Visions of childhood! oft have ye beguiled
Lone manhood's cares, yet waking fondest sighs:
Ah! that once more I were a careless child.

Work Without Hope

All Nature seems at work. Slugs leave their lair—
The bees are stirring—birds are on the wing—
And Winter, slumbering in the open air,
Wears on his smiling face a dream of Spring!
And I, the while, the sole unbusy thing,
Nor honey make, nor pair, nor build, nor sing.
Yet well I ken the banks where amaranths blow,
Have traced the fount where streams of nectar flow.
Bloom, O ye amaranths! bloom for whom ye may,
For me ye bloom not! Glide, rich streams, away!
With lips unbrighten'd, wreathless brow, I stroll:
And would you learn the spells that drowse my soul?
Work without Hope draws nectar in a sieve,
And Hope without an object cannot live.

ROBERT SOUTHEY

Winter

A wrinkled, crabbed man they picture thee,
Old Winter, with a rugged beard as grey
As the long moss upon the apple-tree;
Blue-lipt, an ice-drop at thy sharp blue nose,
Close muffled up, and on thy dreary way
Plodding alone through sleet and drifting snows.
They should have drawn thee by the high-heapt hearth,
Old Winter! seated in thy great armed chair,
Watching the children at their Christmas mirth;
Or circled by them as thy lips declare
Some merry jest, or tale of murder dire,
Or troubled spirit that disturbs the night,
Pausing at times to rouse the mouldering fire,
Or taste the old October brown and bright.

Night and Death

Mysterious Night! when our first parent knew
Thee from report divine, and heard thy name,
Did he not tremble for this lovely frame,
This glorious canopy of light and blue.
Yet 'neath a curtain of translucent dew,
Bathed in the rays of the great setting flame,
Hesperus with the host of heaven came,
And lo! creation widened in man's view.
Who could have thought such darkness lay concealed
Within thy beams, O Sun! or who could find,
Whilst fly and leaf and insect stood revealed,
That to such countless orbs thou mad'st us blind!
Why do we then shun Death with anxious strife?
If Light can thus deceive, wherefore not Life?

CHARLES LAMB

Composed in Hoxton lunatic asylum, Dec. 1795–Jan. 1796

If from my lips some angry accents fell,
Peevish complaint, or harsh reproof unkind,
'Twas but the error of a sickly mind
And troubled thoughts, clouding the purer well,
And waters clear, of Reason; and for me
Let this my verse the poor atonement be—
My verse, which thou to praise wert ever inclined
Too highly, and with a partial eye to see
No blemish. Thou to me didst ever shew
Kindest affection; and would oft-times lend
An ear to the desponding love-sick lay,
Weeping my sorrows with me, who repay
But ill the mighty debt of love I owe,
Mary, to thee, my sister and my friend.

A timid grace sits trembling in her eye

A timid grace sits trembling in her eye,
As loth to meet the rudeness of men's sight,
Yet shedding a delicious lunar light,
That steeps in kind oblivious ecstasy
The care-crazed mind, like some still melody:
Speaking most plain the thoughts which do possess
Her gentle sprite: peace, and meek quietness,
And innocent loves, and maiden purity:
A look whereof might heal the cruel smart
Of changed friends, or fortune's wrongs unkind;
Might to sweet deeds of mercy move the heart
Of him who hates his brethren of mankind.
Turned are those lights from me, who fondly yet
Past joys, vain loves, and buried hopes regret.

The Midnight Wind

O I could laugh to hear the midnight wind,
That, rushing on its way with careless sweep,
Scatters the ocean waves! And I could weep
Like to a child. For now to my raised mind
On wings of winds comes wild-eyed Phantasy,
And her rude visions give severe delight.
O winged bark! how swift along the night
Passed thy proud keel! nor shall I let go by
Lightly of that drear hour the memory,
When wet and chilly on thy deck I stood,
Unbonneted, and gazed upon the flood,
Even till it seemed a pleasant thing to die,—
To be resolved into the elemental wave,
Or take my portion with the winds that rave.

To Dora Wordsworth, on being asked by her Father to Write in her Album

An Album is a banquet; from the store
In his intelligential orchard growing
Your sire might heap your board to overflowing;
One shaking of the tree,—'twould ask no more
To set a salad forth more rich than that
Which Evelyn in his princely cookery fancied,
Or that more rare, by Eve's neat hand enhanced,
Where, a pleased guest, the Angelic Virtue sat.
But like the all-grasping founder of the feast
Whom Nathan to the sinning king did tax,
From his less wealthy neighbours he exacts,
Spares his own flocks, and takes the poor man's beast.
Obedient to his bidding, lo, I am
A zealous, meek, contributory—Lamb.

WALTER SAVAGE LANDOR

To Robert Browning

There is delight in singing, though none hear
Beside the singer; and there is delight
In praising, though the praiser sits alone
And see the prais'd far off him, far above.
Shakespeare is not *our* poet, but the world's,
Therefore on him no speech; and short for thee,
Browning! Since Chaucer was alive and hale,
No man hath walk'd along our roads with step
So active, so inquiring eye, or tongue
So varied in discourse. But warmer climes
Give brighter plumage, stronger wing; the breeze
Of Alpine heights thou playest with, borne on
Beyond Sorento and Amalfi, where
The Siren waits thee, singing song for song.

The Fox-Hunters

What Gods are these? Bright red, or white and green,
Some of them jockey-capp'd and some in hats,
The gods of vermin have their runs, like rats.
Each has six legs, four moving, pendent two,
Like bottled tails, the tilting four between.
Behold Land-Interest's compound Man-and-Horse,
Which so enchants his outraged helot-crew,
Hedge-gapping, with his horn, and view-halloo,
O'er hunter's clover—glorious broom and gorse!
The only crop his godship ever grew:
Except his crop of hate, and smouldering ire,
And cloak'd contempt, of coward insult born,
And hard-faced labour, paid with straw for corn,
And fain to reap it with a scythe of fire.

LEIGH HUNT

To the Grasshopper and the Cricket

Green little vaulter in the sunny grass,
  Catching your heart up at the feel of June,
  Sole voice that's heard amidst the lazy noon,
When even the bees lag at the summoning brass;
And you, warm little housekeeper, who class
  With those who think the candles come too soon,
  Loving the fire, and with your tricksome tune
Nick the glad silent moments as they pass;
O, sweet and tiny cousin! that belong,
  One to the fields, the other to the hearth,
Both have your sunshine; both though small are strong
  At your clear hearts; and both were sent on earth
To sing in thoughtful ears this natural song:
  In doors and out, summer and winter, Mirth.

The Nile

It flows through all hushed Egypt and its sands,
Like some grave mighty thought threading a dream,
And times and things, as in that vision seem
Keeping along it their eternal stands,
Caves, pillars, pyramids, the shepherd bands
That roamed through the young world, the glory extreme
Of high Sesostris, and that southern beam,
The laughing queen that caught the world's great hands.
Then comes a mightier silence, stern and strong,
As of a world left empty of its throng,
And the void weighs on us; and then we wake,
And hear the fruitful stream lapsing along
'Twixt villages, and think how we shall take
Our own calm journey on for human sake.

GEORGE GORDON, LORD BYRON

On Chillon

Eternal Spirit of the chainless Mind!
Brightest in dungeons, Liberty, thou art;
For there thy habitation is the heart,
The heart which love of thee alone can bind;
And when thy sons to fetters are consigned,
To fetters, and the damp vault's dayless gloom,
Their country conquers with their martyrdom,
And Freedom's fame finds wings on every wind.
Chillon! thy prison is a holy place,
And thy sad floor an altar, for 'twas trod,
Until his very steps have left a trace,
Worn, as if thy cold pavement were a sod,
By Bonnivard. May none those marks efface!
For they appeal from tyranny to God.

England in 1819

An old, mad, blind, despised, and dying king,—
Princes, the dregs of their dull race, who flow
Through public scorn,—mud from a muddy spring,—
Rulers who neither see, nor feel, nor know,
But leech-like to their fainting country cling,
Till they drop, blind in blood, without a blow,—
A people starved and stabbed in the untilled field,—
An army, which liberticide and prey
Makes as a two-edged sword to all who wield,—
Golden and sanguine laws which tempt and slay;
Religion Christless, Godless—a book sealed;
A Senate,—Time's worst statute unrepealed,—
Are graves, from which a glorious Phantom may
Burst, to illumine our tempestuous day.

Lift not the painted veil

Lift not the painted veil which those who live
Call Life: though unreal shapes be pictured there,
And it but mimic all we would believe
With colours idly spread,—behind, lurk Fear
And Hope, twin Destinies; who ever weave
Their shadows, o'er the chasm, sightless and drear.
I knew one who had lifted it—he sought,
For his lost heart was tender, things to love,
But found them not, alas! nor was there aught
The world contains, the which he could approve.
Through the unheeding many he did move,
A splendour among shadows, a bright blot
Upon this gloomy scene, a Spirit that strove
For truth, and like the Preacher found it not.

Ye hasten to the dead

Ye hasten to the dead! What seek ye there,
Ye restless thoughts and busy purposes
Of the idle brain, which the world's livery wear?
O thou quick heart which pantest to possess
All that anticipation feigneth fair!
Thou vainly curious mind, which wouldest guess
Whence thou didst come, and whither thou mayst go,
And that which never yet was known wouldst know—
Oh, whither hasten ye, that thus ye press
With such swift feet life's green and pleasant path,
Seeking alike from happiness and woe
A refuge in the cavern of grey death?
O heart, and mind, and thoughts! what thing do you
Hope to inherit in the grave below?

Ozymandias

I met a traveller from an antique land
Who said: Two vast and trunkless legs of stone
Stand in the desert. Near them, on the sand,
Half sunk, a shattered visage lies, whose frown,
And wrinkled lip, and sneer of cold command,
Tell that its sculptor well those passions read
Which yet survive, stamped on these lifeless things,
The hand that mocked them and the heart that fed;
And on the pedestal these words appear:
'My name is Ozymandias, king of kings:
Look on my works, ye Mighty, and despair!'
Nothing beside remains. Round the decay
Of that colossal wreck, boundless and bare
The lone and level sands stretch far away.

At Hooker's Tomb

The grey-eyed Morn was saddened with a shower,
A silent shower, that trickled down so still
Scarce drooped beneath its weight the tenderest flower,
Scarce could you trace it on the twinkling rill,
Or moss-stone bathed in dew. It was an hour
Most meet for prayer beside thy lowly grave,
Most for thanksgiving meet, that Heaven such power
To thy serene and humble spirit gave.
'Who sow good seed with tears shall reap in joy.'
So thought I as I watched the gracious rain,
And deemed it like that silent sad employ
Whence sprung thy glory's harvest, to remain
For ever. God hath sworn to lift on high
Who sinks himself by true humility.

JOHN CLARE

The Happy Bird

The happy white-throat on the swaying bough,
Rocked by the impulse of the gadding wind
That ushers in the showers of April, now
Carols right joyously; and now reclined,
Crouching, she clings close to her moving seat,
To keep her hold;—and till the wind for rest
Pauses, she mutters inward melodies,
That seem her heart's rich thinkings to repeat.
But when the branch is still, her little breast
Swells out in rapture's gushing symphonies;
And then, against her brown wing softly prest,
The wind comes playing, an enraptured guest;
This way and that she swings—till gusts arise
More boisterous in their play, then off she flies.

The Crab-Tree

Spring comes anew, and brings each little pledge
That still, as wont, my childish heart deceives;
I stoop again for violets in the hedge,
Among the ivy and old withered leaves;
And often mark, amid the clumps of sedge,
The pooty-shells I gathered when a boy:
But cares have claimed me many an evil day,
And chilled the relish which I had for joy.
Yet when crab-blossoms blush among the May,
As erst in years gone by, I scramble now
Up 'mid the bramble for my old esteems,
Filling my hands with many a blooming bough;
Till the heart-stirring past as present seems,
Save the bright sunshine of those fairy dreams.

To Dewint

Dewint! I would not flatter, nor would I
Pretend to critic-skill in this thy art;
Yet in thy landscapes I can well descry
The breathing hues as Nature's counterpart.
No painted peaks, no wild romantic sky,
No rocks, nor mountains, as the rich sublime,
Hath made thee famous; but the sunny truth
Of Nature, that doth mark thee for all time,
Found on our level pastures:—spots, forsooth,
Where common skill sees nothing deemed divine;
Yet here a worshipper was found in thee,
And thy young pencil worked such ripe surprise,
That rushy flats, befringed with willow tree,
Rivalled the beauties of Italian skies.

To the Memory of Bloomfield

Sweet unassuming minstrel! not to thee
The dazzling fashions of the day belong;
Nature's wild pictures, field, and cloud, and tree,
And quiet brooks, far distant from the throng,
In murmurs tender as the toiling bee,
Make the sweet music of thy gentle song.
Well! Nature owns thee: let the crowd pass by;
The tide of Fashion is a stream too strong
For pastoral brooks, that gently flow and sing:
But Nature is their source, and earth and sky
Their annual offering to her current bring.
Thy gentle muse and memory need no sigh;
For thine shall murmur on to many a spring,
When prouder streams are summer-burnt and dry.

The Thrush's Nest

Within a thick and spreading hawthorn bush,
That overhung a molehill large and round,
I heard from morn to morn a merry thrush
Sing hymns to sunrise, and I drank the sound
With joy, and, often an intruding guest,
I watched her secret toils from day to day—
How true she warped the moss, to form a nest,
And modelled it within with wood and clay;
And by and by, like heath-bells gilt with dew,
There lay her shining eggs, as bright as flowers,
Ink-spotted-over shells of greeny blue:
And there I witnessed in the sunny hours
A brood of nature's minstrels chirp and fly,
Glad as that sunshine and the laughing sky.

Earth's Eternity

Man, Earth's poor shadow, talks of Earth's decay:
But hath it nothing of eternal kin?
No majesty that shall not pass away?
No soul of greatness springing up within?
Thought-marks without? hoar shadows of sublime
Pictures of power, which if not doomed to win
Eternity, stand laughing at old time
For ages? In the grand ancestral line
Of things eternal, mounting to divine,
I read Magnificence where ages pay
Worship, like conquered foes to the Apennine,
Because they could not conquer. There sits Day
Too high for Night to come at. Mountains shine
Outpeering Time, too lofty for decay.

Burthorp Oak

Old noted oak! I saw thee in a mood
Of vague indifference; and yet with me
Thy memory, like thy fate, hath lingering stood
For years, thou hermit, in the lonely sea
Of grass that waves around thee!—Solitude
Paints not a lonelier picture to the view,
Burthorp! than thy one melancholy tree,
Age-rent, and shattered to a stump. Yet new
Leaves come upon each rift and broken limb
With every spring; and Poesy's visions swim
Around it, of old days and chivalry;
And desolate fancies bid the eyes grow dim
With feelings, that earth's grandeur should decay,
And all its olden memories pass away.

First Sight of Spring

The hazel-blooms, in threads of crimson hue,
Peep through the swelling buds, foretelling Spring,
Ere yet a white-thorn leaf appears in view,
Or March finds throstles pleased enough to sing.
To the old touchwood tree woodpeckers cling
A moment, and their harsh-toned notes renew;
In happier mood, the stockdove claps his wing;
The squirrel sputters up the powdered oak,
With tail cocked o'er his head, and ears erect,
Startled to hear the woodman's understroke;
And with the courage which his fears collect,
He hisses fierce half malice and half glee,
Leaping from branch to branch about the tree,
In winter's foliage, moss and lichens, deckt.

Careless Rambles

I love to wander at my idle will
In summer's joyous prime about the fields,
To kneel when thirsty at the little rill,
And sip the draught its pebbly bottom yields;
And where the maple bush its fountain shields,
To lie, and rest a sultry hour away,
Cropping the swelling peascod from the land;
Or 'mid the sheltering woodland-walks to stray,
Where oaks for aye o'er their old shadows stand;
'Neath whose dark foliage, with a welcome hand,
I pluck the luscious strawberry, ripe and red
As Beauty's lips;—and in my fancy's dreams,
As 'mid the velvet moss I musing tread,
Feel Life as lovely as her picture seems.

On First Looking into Chapman's Homer

Much have I travelled in the realms of gold,
And many goodly states and kingdoms seen;
Round many western islands have I been,
Which bards in fealty to Apollo hold.
Oft of one wide expanse had I been told,
That deep-browed Homer ruled as his demesne;
Yet did I never breathe its pure serene
Till I heard Chapman speak out loud and bold:
Then felt I like some watcher of the skies
When a new planet swims into his ken,
Or like stout Cortez, when, with eagle eyes,
He stared at the Pacific—and all his men
Looked at each other with a wild surmise—
Silent, upon a peak in Darien.

To Sleep

O soft embalmer of the still midnight!
Shutting, with careful fingers and benign,
Our gloom-pleased eyes, embowered from the light,
Enshaded in forgetfulness divine:
O soothest Sleep! if so it please thee, close,
In midst of this mine hymn, my willing eyes,
Or wait the amen, ere thy poppy throws
Around my head its lulling charities;
Then save me, or the passed day will shine
Upon my pillow, breeding many woes;
Save me from curious conscience, that still lords
Its strength, for darkness burrowing like a mole:
Turn the key deftly in the oiled wards,
And seal the hushed casket of my soul.

To Ailsa Rock

Hearken, thou craggy ocean pyramid!
Give answer from thy voice, the sea-fowls' screams!
When were thy shoulders mantled in huge streams?
When, from the sun, was thy broad forehead hid?
How long is't since the mighty power bid
Thee heave to airy sleep from fathom dreams?
Sleep in the lap of thunder or sunbeams,
Or, when grey clouds are thy cold cover-lid?
Thou answer'st not, for thou art dead asleep!
Thy life is but two dead eternities—
The last in air, the former in the deep;
First with the whales, last with the eagle-skies—
Drown'd wast thou till an earthquake made thee sleep,
Another cannot wake thy giant size.

On Fame

'You cannot eat your cake and have it too.'—Proverb

How fever'd is the man, who cannot look
Upon his mortal days with temperate blood,
Who vexes all the leaves of his life's book,
And robs his fair name of its maidenhood;
It is as if the rose should pluck herself,
Or the ripe plum finger its misty bloom,
As if a Naiad, like a meddling elf,
Should darken her pure grot with muddy gloom;
But the rose leaves herself upon the briar,
For winds to kiss and grateful bees to feed,
And the ripe plum still wears its dim attire;
The undisturbed lake has crystal space;
Why then should man, teasing the world for grace,
Spoil his salvation for a fierce miscreed?

Why did I laugh to-night?

Why did I laugh to-night? No voice will tell:
No God, no Demon of severe response,
Deigns to reply from Heaven or from Hell.
Then to my human heart I turn at once.
Heart! Thou and I are here, sad and alone;
I say, why did I laugh? O mortal pain!
O Darkness! Darkness! ever must I moan,
To question Heaven and Hell and Heart in vain.
Why did I laugh? I know this Being's lease,
My fancy to its utmost blisses spreads;
Yet would I on this very midnight cease,
And the world's gaudy ensigns see in shreds;
Verse, Fame, and Beauty are intense indeed,
But Death intenser—Death is Life's high meed.

If by dull rhymes our English must be chain'd

If by dull rhymes our English must be chain'd,
And, like Andromeda, the Sonnet sweet
Fetter'd, in spite of pained loveliness;
Let us find out, if we must be constrain'd,
Sandals more interwoven and complete
To fit the naked foot of poesy;
Let us inspect the lyre, and weigh the stress
Of every chord, and see what may be gain'd
By ear industrious, and attention meet;
Misers of sound and syllable, no less
Than Midas of his coinage, let us be
Jealous of dead leaves in the bay wreath crown;
So, if we may not let the Muse be free,
She will be bound with garlands of her own.

To Homer

Standing aloof in giant ignorance,
Of thee I hear, and of the Cyclades,
As one who sits ashore, and longs perchance
To visit dolphin-coral in deep seas.
So thou wast blind!—but then the veil was rent,
For Jove uncurtained Heaven to let thee live,
And Neptune made for thee a spermy tent,
And Pan made sing for thee his forest-hive.
Ay, on the shores of darkness there is light,
And precipices show untrodden green;
There is a budding morrow in midnight;
There is a triple sight in blindness keen;
Such seeing hadst thou, as it once befell
To Dian, Queen of Earth, and Heaven, and Hell.

After dark vapours have oppress'd our plains

After dark vapours have oppress'd our plains
For a long dreary season, comes a day
Born of the gentle South, and clears away
From the sick heavens all unseemly stains.
The anxious month, relieved from its pains,
Takes as a long-lost right the feel of May,
The eye-lids with the passing coolness play,
Like rose-leaves with the drip of summer rains.
And calmest thoughts come round us—as of leaves
Budding—fruit ripening in stillness—autumn suns
Smiling at eve upon the quiet sheaves,—
Sweet Sappho's cheek,—a sleeping infant's breath,—
The gradual sand that through an hour-glass runs,—
A woodland rivulet,—a Poet's death.

On the Elgin Marbles

My spirit is too weak; mortality
Weighs heavily on me like unwilling sleep,
And each imagined pinnacle and steep
Of Godlike hardship tells me I must die
Like a sick eagle looking at the sky.
Yet 'tis a gentle luxury to weep,
That I have not the cloudy winds to keep
Fresh for the opening of the morning's eye.
Such dim-conceived glories of the brain
Bring round the heart an indescribable feud;
So do these wonders a most dizzy pain,
That mingles Grecian grandeur with the rude
Wasting of old Time—with a billowy main
A sun, a shadow of a magnitude.

When I have fears that I may cease to be

When I have fears that I may cease to be
Before my pen has gleaned my teeming brain,
Before high-piled books, in charact'ry
Hold like rich garners the full-ripened grain;
When I behold, upon the night's starred face,
Huge cloudy symbols of a high romance,
And think that I may never live to trace
Their shadows, with the magic hand of chance;
And when I feel, fair creature of an hour!
That I shall never look upon thee more,
Never have relish in the faery power
Of unreflecting love!—then on the shore
Of the wide world I stand alone, and think
Till Love and Fame to nothingness do sink.

Last Sonnet—Written on a blank page in Shakespeare's 'Poems', facing 'A Lover's Complaint'

Bright star, would I were steadfast as thou art—
  Not in lone splendour hung aloft the night
And watching, with eternal lids apart,
  Like Nature's patient, sleepless Eremite,
The moving waters at their priestlike task
  Of pure ablution round earth's human shores,
Or gazing on the new soft-fallen mask
  Of snow upon the mountains and the moors—
No—yet still steadfast, still unchangeable,
  Pillow'd upon my fair love's ripening breast,
To feel for ever its soft fall and swell,
  Awake for ever in a sweet unrest,
Still, still to hear her tender-taken breath,
And so live ever—or else swoon to death.

HARTLEY COLERIDGE

If I have sinned in act, I may repent

If I have sinned in act, I may repent;
If I have erred in thought, I may disclaim
My silent error, and yet feel no shame:
But if my soul, big with an ill intent,
Guilty in will, by fate be innocent,
Or being bad, yet murmurs at the curse
And incapacity of being worse,
That makes my hungry passion still keep Lent
In keen expectance of a Carnival,—
Where, in all worlds that round the sun revolve,
And shed their influence on this passive ball,
Abides a power that can my soul absolve?
Could any sin survive and be forgiven,
One sinful wish would make a hell of heaven.

To a Friend

When we were idlers with the loitering rills,
The need of human love we little noted:
Our love was nature; and the peace that floated
On the white mist, and dwelt upon the hills,
To sweet accord subdued our wayward wills:
One soul was ours, one mind, one heart devoted,
That, wisely doating, asked not why it doated,
And ours the unknown joy, which knowing kills.
But now I find how dear thou wert to me;
That man is more than half of nature's treasure,
Of that fair beauty which no eye can see,
Of that sweet music which no ear can measure;
And now the streams may sing for others' pleasure,
The hills sleep on in their eternity.

Long time a child

Long time a child, and still a child, when years
Had painted manhood on my cheek, was I,—
For yet I lived like one not born to die;
A thriftless prodigal of smiles and tears,
No hope I needed, and I knew no fears.
But sleep, though sweet, is only sleep; and waking,
I waked to sleep no more; at once o'ertaking
The vanguard of my age, with all arrears
Of duty on my back. Nor child, nor man,
Nor youth, nor sage, I find my head is gray,
For I have lost the race I never ran:
A rathe December blights my lagging May;
And still I am a child, though I be old:
Time is my debtor for my years untold.

Let me not deem that I was made in vain

Let me not deem that I was made in vain,
Or that my being was an accident
Which Fate, in working its sublime intent,
Not wished to be, to hinder would not deign.
Each drop uncounted in a storm of rain
Hath its own mission, and is duly sent
To its own leaf or blade, not idly spent
'Mid myriad dimples on the shipless main.
The very shadow of an insect's wing,
For which the violet cared not while it stayed,
Yet felt the lighter for its vanishing,
Proved that the sun was shining by its shade.
Then can a drop of the eternal spring,
Shadow of living lights, in vain be made?

Prayer

i

There is an awful quiet in the air,
And the sad earth, with moist imploring eye,
Looks wide and wakeful at the pondering sky,
Like Patience slow subsiding to Despair.
But see, the blue smoke as a voiceless prayer,
Sole witness of a secret sacrifice,
Unfolds its tardy wreaths, and multiplies
Its soft chameleon breathings in the rare
Capacious ether,—so it fades away,
And nought is seen beneath the pendent blue,
The undistinguishable waste of day.
So have I dreamed!—oh, may the dream be true!—
That praying souls are purged from mortal hue,
And grow as pure as He to whom they pray.

ii

Be not afraid to pray—to pray is right.
Pray, if thou canst, with hope; but ever pray,
Though hope be weak, or sick with long delay;
Pray in the darkness, if there be no light.
Far is the time, remote from human site
When war and discord on the earth shall cease;
Yet every prayer for universal peace
Avails the blessed time to expedite.
Whate'er is good to wish, ask that of Heaven,
Though it be what thou canst not hope to see:
Pray to be perfect, though material leaven
Forbid the spirit so on earth to be;
But if for any wish thou darest not pray,
Then pray to God to cast that wish away.

Full well I know

Full well I know—my Friends—ye look on me
A living spectre of my Father dead—
Had I not borne his name, had I not fed
On him, as one leaf trembling on a tree,
A woeful waste had been my minstrelsy—
Yet have I sung of maidens newly wed
And I have wished that hearts too sharply bled
Should throb with less of pain, and heave more free
But my endeavour. Still alone I sit
Counting each thought as Miser counts a penny,
Wishing to spend my penny-worth of wit
On antic wheel of fortune like a Zany:
You love me for my sire, to you unknown,
Revere me for his sake, and love me for my own.

Night

The crackling embers on the hearth are dead;
The indoor note of industry is still;
The latch is fast; upon the window sill
The small birds wait not for their daily bread;
The voiceless flowers—how quietly they shed
Their nightly odours;—and the household rill
Murmurs continuous dulcet sounds that fill
The vacant expectation, and the dread
Of listening night. And haply now she sleeps;
For all the garrulous noises of the air
Are hush'd in peace; the soft dew silent weeps,
Like hopeless lovers for a maid so fair—
Oh! that I were the happy dream that creeps
To her soft heart, to find my image there.

Think upon Death

Think upon Death, 'tis good to think of Death,
But better far to think upon the Dead.
Death is a spectre with a bony head,
Or the mere mortal body without breath,
The state foredoomed of every son of Seth,
Decomposition—dust, or dreamless sleep.
But the dear Dead are they for whom we weep,
For whom I credit all the Bible saith.
Dead is my father, dead is my good mother,
And what on earth have I to do but die?
But if by grace I reach the blessed sky,
I fain would see the same, and not another;
The very father that I used to see,
The mother that has nursed me on her knee.

Silence

There is a silence where hath been no sound,
  There is a silence where no sound may be,
  In the cold grave—under the deep deep sea,
Or in wide desert where no life is found,
Which hath been mute, and still must sleep profound;
  No voice is hush'd—no life treads silently,
  But clouds and cloudy shadows wander free,
That never spoke, over the idle ground:
But in green ruins, in the desolate walls
  Of antique palaces, where Man hath been,
Though the dun fox, or wild hyaena, calls,
  And owls, that flit continually between,
Shriek to the echo, and the low winds moan,
There the true Silence is, self-conscious and alone.

Death

It is not death, that sometime in a sigh
  This eloquent breath shall take its speechless flight;
That sometime these bright stars, that now reply
  In sunlight to the sun, shall set in night,
  That this warm conscious flesh shall perish quite,
And all life's ruddy springs forget to flow;
  That thoughts shall cease, and the immortal sprite
Be lapped in alien clay and laid below;
It is not death to know this,—but to know
  That pious thoughts, which visit at new graves
In tender pilgrimage, will cease to go
  So duly and so oft,—and when grass waves
Over the past-away, there may be then
  No resurrection in the minds of men.

Leaves

Leaves of the summer, lovely summer's pride,
  Sweet is the shade below your silent tree,
Whether in waving copses, where ye hide
  My roamings, or in fields that let me see
  The open sky; and whether ye may be
Around the low-stemm'd oak, robust and wide;
Or taper ash upon the mountain side;
  Or lowland elm; your shade is sweet to me.

Whether ye wave above the early flow'rs
  In lively green; or whether, rustling sere,
Ye fly on playful winds, around my feet,

In dying autumn; lovely are your bow'rs,
  Ye early-dying children of the year;
    Holy the silence of your calm retreat.

JOHN HENRY NEWMAN

Substance and Shadow

'Man walketh in a vain shadow, and disquieteth himself in vain.'

They do but grope in learning's pedant round,
Who on the fantasies of sense bestow
An idol substance, bidding us bow low
Before those shades of being which are found
Stirring or still on man's brief trial ground;
As if such shapes and moods, which come and go,
Had aught of Truth or Life in their poor show,
To sway or judge, and skill to sain or wound.
Son of immortal Seed, high destined Man!
Know thy dread gift,—a creature, yet a cause;
Each mind is its own centre, and it draws
Home to itself, and moulds in its thought's span
All outward things, the vassals of its will,
Aided by Heaven, by earth unthwarted still.

Melchizedek

'Without father, without mother, without descent, having neither beginning of days, nor end of life.'

Thrice blest are they who feel their loneliness;
To whom nor voice of friend nor pleasant scene
Brings that on which the saddened heart can lean;
Yea, the rich earth, garbed in its daintiest dress
Of light and joy, doth but the more oppress,
Claiming responsive smiles and rapture high:
Till, sick at heart, beyond the veil they fly,
Seeking His presence, who alone can bless.
Such, in strange days, the weapons of Heaven's grace
When, passing o'er the high-born Hebrew line,
He forms the vessel of his vast design;
Fatherless, homeless, reft of age and place,
Severed from earth, and careless of its wreck,
Born through long woe His rare Melchizedek.

THOMAS LOVELL BEDDOES

To Tartar, A Terrier Beauty

Snow-drop of dogs, with ear of brownest dye,
Like the last orphan leaf of naked tree
Which shudders in bleak autumn; though by thee,
Of hearing careless and untutored eye,
Not understood articulate speech of men,
Nor marked the artificial mind of books,
—The mortal's voice eternized by the pen,—
Yet hast thou thought and language all unknown
To Babel's scholars; oft intensest looks,
Long scrutiny o'er some dark-veined stone
Dost thou bestow, learning dead mysteries
Of the world's birth-day, oft in eager tone
With quick-tailed fellows bandiest prompt replies,
Solicitudes canine, four-footed amities.

The Lamp

As yonder lamp in my vacated room
  With arduous flame disputes the darksome night,
  And can, with its involuntary light,
But lifeless things, that near it stand, illume;
Yet all the while it doth itself consume,
  And, ere the sun begins its heavenly height
  With courier beams that meet the shepherd's sight,
There, whence its life arose, shall be its tomb—

So wastes my light away. Perforce confined
  To common things, a limit to its sphere,
It shines on worthless trifles undesign'd
  With fainter ray each hour imprison'd here.
Alas! to know that the consuming mind
  Shall leave its lamp cold, ere the sun appear.

ROBERT STEPHEN HAWKER

Pater Vester Pascit Illa

Our bark is on the waters! wide around
The wandering wave; above, the lonely sky:
Hush! a young sea-bird floats, and that quick cry
Shrieks to the levelled weapon's echoing sound:
Grasps its lank wing, and on, with reckless bound!
Yet, creature of the surf, a sheltering breast
To-night shall haunt in vain thy far-off nest,
A call unanswered search the rocky ground.
Lord of leviathan! when Ocean heard
Thy gathering voice, and sought his native breeze;
When whales first plunged with life, and the proud deep
Felt unborn tempests heave in troubled sleep,
Thou didst provide, even for this nameless bird,
Home and a natural love amid the surging seas.

Finite and Infinite

The wind sounds only in opposing straits,
The sea, beside the shore; man's spirit rends
Its quiet only up against the ends
Of wants and oppositions, loves and hates,
Where, worked and worn by passionate debates,
And losing by the loss it apprehends,
The flesh rocks round, and every breath it sends
Is ravelled to a sigh. All tortured states
Suppose a straitened place. Jehovah Lord,
Make room for rest, around me! out of sight
Now float me, of the vexing land abhorred,
Till in deep calms of space my soul may right
Her nature,—shoot large sail on lengthening cord,
And rush exultant on the Infinite.

And wilt thou have me fashion

And wilt thou have me fashion into speech
The love I bear thee, finding words enough,
And hold the torch out, while the winds are rough,
Between our faces, to cast light on each?—
I drop it at thy feet. I cannot teach
My hand to hold my spirit so far off
From myself . . . me . . . that I should bring thee proof
In words, of love hid in me out of reach.
Nay, let the silence of my womanhood
Commend my woman-love to thy belief,—
Seeing that I stand unwon, however wooed,
And rend the garment of my life, in brief,
By a most dauntless, voiceless fortitude,
Lest one touch of this heart convey its grief.

If thou must love me

If thou must love me, let it be for nought
Except for love's sake only. Do not say
'I love her for her smile . . . her look . . . her way
Of speaking gently, . . . for a trick of thought
That falls in well with mine, and certes brought
A sense of pleasant ease on such a day'—
For these things in themselves, Beloved, may
Be changed, or change for thee,—and love, so wrought,
May be unwrought so. Neither love me for
Thine own dear pity's wiping my cheeks dry,—
A creature might forget to weep, who bore
Thy comfort long, and lose thy love thereby!
But love me for love's sake, that evermore
Thou mayst love on, through love's eternity.

The Soul's Expression

With stammering lips and insufficient sound
I strive and struggle to deliver right
That music of my nature, day and night
With dream and thought and feeling interwound,
And inly answering all the senses round
With octaves of a mystic depth and height
Which step out grandly to the infinite
From the dark edges of the sensual ground!
This song of soul I struggle to outbear
Through portals of the sense, sublime and whole,
And utter all myself into the air.
But if I did it,—as the thunder-roll
Breaks its own cloud, my flesh would perish there,
Before that dread apocalypse of soul.

Past and Future

My future will not copy fair my past
On any leaf but Heaven's. Be fully done,
Supernal Will! I would not fain be one
Who, satisfying thirst and breaking fast
Upon the fullness of the heart, at last
Says no grace after meat. My wine has run
Indeed out of my cup, and there is none
To gather up the bread of my repast
Scattered and trampled,—yet I find some good
In earth's green herbs, and streams that bubble up
Clear from the darkling ground,—content until
I sit with angels before better food.
Dear Christ! when Thy new vintage fills my cup,
This hand shall shake no more, nor that wine spill.

Grief

I tell you, hopeless grief is passionless;
That only men incredulous of despair,
Half-taught in anguish, through the midnight air
Beat upward to God's throne in loud access
Of shrieking and reproach. Full desertness
In souls, as countries, lieth silent-bare
Under the blanching, vertical eye-glare
Of the absolute Heavens. Deep-hearted man, express
Grief for thy Dead in silence like to death:—
Most like a monumental statue set
In everlasting watch and moveless woe,
Till itself crumble to the dust beneath.
Touch it: the marble eyelids are not wet;
If it could weep, it could arise and go.

How do I love thee?

How do I love thee? let me count the ways.
I love thee to the depth and breadth and height
My soul can reach, when feeling out of sight
For the ends of Being and Ideal Grace.
I love thee to the level of every day's
Most quiet need, by sun and candlelight.
I love thee freely, as men strive for Right;
I love thee purely, as they turn from Praise;
I love thee with the passion put to use
In my old griefs, and with my childhood's faith;
I love thee with a love I seemed to lose
With my lost saints,—I love thee with the breath,
Smiles, tears, of all my life!—and, if God choose,
I shall but love thee better after death.

HENRY WADSWORTH LONGFELLOW

Chaucer

An old man in a lodge within a park;
  The chamber walls depicted all around
  With portraitures of huntsman, hawk, and hound,
  And the hurt deer. He listeneth to the lark,
Whose song comes with the sunshine through the dark
  Of painted glass in leaden lattice bound;
  He listeneth and he laugheth at the sound,
  Then writeth in a book like any clerk.
He is the poet of the dawn, who wrote
  The Canterbury Tales, and his old age
  Made beautiful with song; and as I read
I hear the crowing cock, I hear the note
  Of lark and linnet, and from every page
  Rise odors of ploughed field or flowery mead.

The Cross of Snow

In the long, sleepless watches of the night,
  A gentle face—the face of one long dead—
  Looks at me from the wall, where round its head
  The night-lamp casts a halo of pale light.
Here in this room she died; and soul more white
  Never through martyrdom of fire was led
  To its repose; nor can in books be read
  The legend of a life more benedight.
There is a mountain in the distant West
  That, sun-defying, in its deep ravines
  Displays a cross of snow upon its side.
Such is the cross I wear upon my breast
  These eighteen years, through all the changing scenes
  And seasons, changeless since the day she died.

Autumn

Thou comest, Autumn, heralded by the rain,
  With banners, by great gales incessant fann'd,
  Brighter than brightest silks of Samarcand,
  And stately oxen harness'd to thy wain;
Thou standest, like imperial Charlemagne,
  Upon thy bridge of gold; thy royal hand
  Outstretched with benedictions o'er the land,
  Blessing the farms through all thy vast domain.
Thy shield is the red harvest moon, suspended
  So long beneath the heaven's o'erhanging eaves;
Thy steps are by the farmer's prayers attended;
  Like flames upon an altar shine the sheaves;
And, following thee, in thy ovation splendid,
  Thine almoner, the wind, scatters the golden leaves!

Divina Commedia

Oft have I seen at some cathedral door
  A laborer, pausing in the dust and heat,
  Lay down his burden, and with reverent feet
  Enter, and cross himself, and on the floor
Kneel to repeat his paternoster o'er;
  Far off the noises of the world retreat;
  The loud vociferations of the street
  Become an undistinguishable roar.
So, as I enter here from day to day,
  And leave my burden at this minster gate,
  Kneeling in prayer, and not ashamed to pray,
The tumult of the time disconsolate
  To inarticulate murmurs dies away,
  While the eternal ages watch and wait.

CHARLES TENNYSON TURNER

Letty's Globe

When Letty had scarce passed her third glad year,
And her young artless words began to flow,
One day we gave the child a coloured sphere
Of the wide earth, that she might mark and know,
By tint and outline, all its sea and land.
She patted all the world; old empires peeped
Between her baby fingers. Her soft hand
Was welcome at all frontiers. How she leaped,
And laughed, and prattled, in her world-wide bliss.
But when we turned her sweet unlearned eye
On our own isle, she raised a joyous cry,
'Oh! yes, I see it. Letty's home is there!'
And while she hid all England with a kiss,
Bright over Europe fell her golden hair.

To Beatrice on her First Interview with Dante

Daughter of Portinari, thou hast met
This eve the bard of Hell and Paradise.
By love's own hand the very hour was set
For thy glad greeting, and his sweet surprise.
In that short interview his loving eye
Hath seized thy fair belongings, and distrained
Thy crimson gown to dress his dreams with joy,
And flame across his lonely hours. He gained
A prize in meeting thee, and thou hast part
Henceforth in him, to all his fame allied,
For thou hast passed into a poet's heart,
To be his Beatrice, his angel guide.
Hail, little handmaid of a great renown,
With thine eight summers, and thy crimson gown.

The Steam Threshing-Machine, with the Straw Carrier

Flush with the pond the lurid furnace burned
At eve, while smoke and vapour filled the yard;
The gloomy winter sky was dimly starred,
The fly-wheel with a mellow murmur turned;
While, ever rising on its mystic stair
In the dim light, from secret chambers borne,
The straw of harvest, severed from the corn,
Climbed, and fell over, in the murky air.
I thought of mind and matter, will and law,
And then of him, who set his stately seal
Of Roman words on all the forms he saw
Of old-world husbandry: *I* could but feel
With what a rich precision *he* would draw
The endless ladder, and the booming wheel!

On the Eclipse of the Moon of October 1865

One little noise of life remained—I heard
The train pause in the distance, then rush by,
Brawling and hushing, like some busy fly
That murmurs and then settles; nothing stirred
Beside. The shadow of our travelling earth
Hung on the silver moon, which mutely went
Through that grand process, without token sent,
Or any sign to call a gazer forth,
Had I not chanced to see; dumb was the vault
Of heaven, and dumb the fields—no zephyr swept
The forest walks, or through the coppice crept;
Nor other sound the stillness did assault,
Save that faint-brawling railway's move and halt;
So perfect was the silence Nature kept.

EDGAR ALLAN POE

To Science

Science! true daughter of Old Time thou art!
  Who alterest all things with thy peering eyes.
Why preyest thou thus upon the poet's heart,
  Vulture, whose wings are dull realities?
How should he love thee? or how deem thee wise,
  Who wouldst not leave him in his wandering
To seek her treasure in the jewelled skies,
  Albeit he soared with an undaunted wing?
Hast thou not dragged Diana from her car,
  And driven the Hamadryad from the wood
To seek a shelter in some happier star?
  Hast thou not torn the Naiad from her flood,
The Elfin from the green grass, and from me
The summer dream beneath the tamarind tree?

Prefatory Sonnet to the 'Nineteenth Century'

Those that of late had flitted far and fast
  To touch all shores, now leaving to the skill
  Of others their old craft seaworthy still,
Have charted this; where, mindful of the past,
Our true co-mates regather round the mast;
  Of diverse tongue, but with a common will
  Here in this roaring moon of daffodil
And crocus, to put forth and brave the blast;
For some, descending from the sacred peak
  Of hoar high-templed Faith, have leagued again
  Their lot with ours to rove the world about;
And some are wilder comrades, sworn to seek
  If any golden harbour be for men
    In seas of Death and sunless gulfs of Doubt.

The pallid thunder-stricken

The pallid thunder-stricken sigh for gain,
Down an ideal stream they ever float,
And sailing on Pactolus in a boat,
Drown soul and sense, while wistfully they strain
Weak eyes upon the glistering sands that robe
The understream. The wise, could he behold
Cathedralled caverns of thick-ribbed gold
And branching silvers of the central globe,
Would marvel from so beautiful a sight
How scorn and ruin, pain and hate could flow:
But Hatred in a gold cave sits below;
Pleached with her hair, in mail of argent light
Shot into gold, a snake her forehead clips,
And skins the colour from her trembling lips.

Eyes calm beside thee

Eyes, calm beside thee, (Lady, could'st thou know!)
  May turn away thick with fast-gathering tears:
I glance not where all gaze: thrilling and low
  Their passionate praises reach thee—my cheek wears
Alone no wonder when thou passest by;
Thy tremulous lids bent and suffused reply
To the irrepressible homage which doth glow
  On every lip but mine: if in thine ears
Their accents linger—and thou dost recall
  Me as I stood, still, guarded, very pale,
Beside each votarist whose lighted brow
Wore worship like an aureole, 'O'er them all
  My beauty,' thou wilt murmur, 'did prevail
Save that one only:' —Lady, could'st thou know!

Now

Out of your whole life give but a moment!
All of your life that has gone before,
All to come after it,—so you ignore,
So you make perfect the present,—condense,
In a rapture of rage, for perfection's endowment,
Thought and feeling and soul and sense—
Merged in a moment which gives me at last
You around me for once, you beneath me, above me—
Me—sure that despite of time future, time past,—
This tick of our life-time's one moment you love me!
How long such suspension may linger? Ah, Sweet—
The moment eternal—just that and no more—
When ecstasy's utmost we clutch at the core
While cheeks burn, arms open, eyes shut and lips meet!

The Hand and Foot

The hand and foot that stir not, they shall find
Sooner than all the rightful place to go:
Now in their motion free as roving wind,
Though first no snail so limited and slow;
I mark them full of labor all the day,
Each active motion made in perfect rest;
They cannot from their path mistaken stray,
Though 't is not theirs, yet in it they are blest;
The bird has not their hidden track found out,
The cunning fox though full of art he be;
It is the way unseen, the certain route,
Where ever bound, yet thou art ever free;
The path of Him, whose perfect law of love
Bids spheres and atoms in just order move.

Yourself

'Tis to yourself I speak; you cannot know
Him whom I call in speaking such a one,
For you beneath the ground lie buried low,
Which he alone as living walks upon:
You may at times have heard him speak to you,
And often wished perchance that you were he;
And I must ever wish that it were true,
For then you could hold fellowship with me:
But now you hear us talk as strangers, met
Above the room wherein you lie abed;
A word perhaps loud spoken you may get,
Or hear our feet when heavily they tread;
But he who speaks, or him who's spoken to,
Must both remain as strangers still to you.

The Garden

I saw the spot where our first parents dwelt;
And yet it wore to me no face of change,
For while amid its fields and groves, I felt
As if I had not sinned, nor thought it strange;
My eye seemed but a part of every sight,
My ear heard music in each sound that rose;
Each sense forever found a new delight,
Such as the spirit's vision only knows;
Each act some new and ever-varying joy
Did by my Father's love for me prepare;
To dress the spot my ever fresh employ,
And in the glorious whole with Him to share;
No more within the flaming gate to stray,
No more for sin's dark stain the debt of death to pay.

In Him We Live

Father! I bless thy name that I do live,
And in each motion am made rich with Thee,
That when a glance is all that I can give,
It is a kingdom's wealth, if I but see;
This stately body cannot move, save I
Will to its nobleness my little bring;
My voice its measured cadence will not try,
Save I with every note consent to sing;
I cannot raise my hands to hurt or bless,
But I with every action must conspire
To show me there how little I possess,
And yet that little more than I desire;
May each new act my new allegiance prove,
Till in thy perfect love I ever live and move.

The Latter Rain

The latter rain,—it falls in anxious haste
Upon the sun-dried fields and branches bare,
Loosening with searching drops the rigid waste,
As if it would each root's lost strength repair;
But not a blade grows green as in the spring,
No swelling twig puts forth its thickening leaves;
The robins only mid the harvests sing,
Pecking the grain that scatters from the sheaves:
The rain falls still,—the fruit all ripened drops,
It pierces chestnut burr and walnut shell,
The furrowed fields disclose the yellow crops,
Each bursting pod of talents used can tell,
And all that once received the early rain
Declare to man it was not sent in vain.

The Dead

I see them,—crowd on crowd they walk the earth,
Dry leafless trees no autumn wind laid bare;
And in their nakedness find cause for mirth,
And all unclad would winter's rudeness dare;
No sap doth through their clattering branches flow,
Whence springing leaves and blossoms bright appear;
Their hearts the living God have ceased to know
Who gives the spring-time to th' expectant year.
They mimic life, as if from Him to steal
His glow of health to paint the livid cheek;
They borrow words for thoughts they cannot feel,
That with a seeming heart their tongue may speak;
And in their show of life more dead they live
Than those that to the earth with many tears they give.

The Earth

I would lie low—the ground on which men tread—
Swept by thy Spirit like the wind of heaven;
An earth, where gushing springs and corn for bread
By me at every season should be given;
Yet not the water or the bread that now
Supplies their tables with its daily food,
But they should gather fruit from every bough,
Such as Thou givest me, and call it good;
And water from the stream of life should flow,
By every dwelling that thy love has built,
Whose taste the ransomed of thy Son shall know,
Whose robes are washed from every stain of guilt;
And men would own it was thy hand that blest,
And from my bosom find a surer rest.

Thy Brother's Blood

I have no brother,—they who meet me now
Offer a hand with their own wills defiled,
And, while they wear a smooth unwrinkled brow,
Know not that Truth can never be beguiled;
Go wash the hand that still betrays thy guilt;—
Before the spirit's gaze what stain can hide?
Abel's red blood upon the earth is spilt,
And by thy tongue it cannot be denied;
I hear not with the ear,—the heart doth tell
Its secret deeds to me untold before;
Go, all its hidden plunder quickly sell,
Then shalt thou cleanse thee from thy brother's gore,
Then will I take thy gift;—that bloody stain
Shall not be seen upon thy hand again.

The Sun God

I saw the Master of the Sun. He stood
  High in his luminous car, himself more bright;
  An Archer of immeasurable might:
On his left shoulder hung his quiver'd load;
Spurn'd by his steeds the eastern mountains glowed;
  Forward his eagle eye and bow of Light
He bent, and while both hands that arch embowed,
  Shaft after shaft pursued the flying night.
No wings profaned that godlike form: around
  His neck high held an ever-moving crowd
Of locks hung glistening: while such perfect sound
  Fell from his bowstring that th' ethereal dome
Thrilled as a dew-drop; and each passing cloud
  Expanded, whitening like the ocean foam.

ARTHUR HUGH CLOUGH

Blank Misgivings of a Creature moving about in Worlds not realised

i

Here am I yet, another twelvemonth spent,
One-third departed of the mortal span,
Carrying on the child into the man,
Nothing into reality. Sails rent,
And rudder broken,—reason impotent,—
Affections all unfixed; so forth I fare
On the mid seas unheedingly, so dare
To do and to be done by, well content.
So was it from the first, so is it yet;
Yea, the first kiss that by these lips was set
On any human lips, methinks was sin—
Sin, cowardice, and falsehood; for the will
Into a deed e'en then advanced, wherein
God, unidentified, was thought-of still.

ii

Though to the vilest things beneath the moon
For poor Ease' sake I give away my heart,
And for the moment's sympathy let part
My sight and sense of truth, Thy precious boon,
My painful earnings, lost, all lost, as soon,
Almost, as gained; and though aside I start,
Belie Thee daily, hourly,—still Thou art,
Art surely as in heaven the sun at noon;
How much so e'er I sin, whate'er I do
Of evil, still the sky above is blue,
The stars look down in beauty as before:
It is enough to walk as best we may,
To walk, and, sighing, dream, of that blest day
When ill we cannot quell shall be no more.

iii

Well, well,—Heaven bless you all from day to day!
Forgiveness too, or e'er we part, from each,
As I do give it, so must I beseech:
I owe all much, much more than I can pay;
Therefore it is I go; how could I stay
Where every look commits me to fresh debt,
And to pay little I must borrow yet?
Enough of this already, now away!
With silent woods and hills untenanted
Let me go commune; under thy sweet gloom,
O kind maternal Darkness, hide my head:
The day may come I yet may re-assume
My place, and, these tired limbs recruited, seek
The task for which I now am all too weak.

iv

Yes, I have lied, and so must walk my way,
Bearing the liar's curse upon my head;
Letting my weak and sickly heart be fed
On food which does the present craving stay,
But may be clean-denied me e'en to-day,
And tho' 'twere certain, yet were ought but bread;
Letting—for so they say, it seems, I said,
And I am all too weak to disobey!
Therefore for me sweet Nature's scenes reveal not
Their charm; sweet Music greets me and I feel not
Sweet eyes pass off me uninspired; yea, more,
The golden tide of opportunity
Flows wafting in friendships and better,—I
Unseeing, listless, pace along the shore.

MATTHEW ARNOLD

Shakespeare

Others abide our question. Thou art free.
We ask and ask. Thou smilest and art still,
Out-topping knowledge. For the loftiest hill
Who to the stars uncrowns his majesty,
Planting his steadfast footsteps in the sea,
Making the heaven of heavens his dwelling-place,
Spears but the cloudy border of his base
To the foiled searching of mortality.
And thou, who didst the stars and sunbeams know,
Self-schooled, self-scanned, self-honoured, self-secure,
Didst tread on earth unguessed at. Better so!
All pains the immortal spirit must endure,
All weakness which impairs, all griefs which bow,
Find their sole speech in that victorious brow.

Written in Butler's Sermons

Affections, instincts, principles and powers,
Impulse and reason, freedom and control—
So men, unravelling God's harmonious whole,
Rend in a thousand shreds this life of ours.
Vain labour! Deep and broad, where none may see,
Spring the foundations of that shadowy throne,
Where man's one nature, queen-like, sits alone,
Centred in a majestic unity,
And rays her powers, like sister-islands, seen
Linking their coral arms under the sea,
Or clustered peaks with plunging gulfs between,
Spanned by aerial arches all of gold,
Whereo'er the chariot wheels of life are rolled
In cloudy circles, to Eternity.

COVENTRY PATMORE

My childhood

My childhood was a vision heavenly wrought;
  High joys of which I sometimes dream, yet fail
  To recollect sufficient to bewail,
And now for ever seek, came then unsought:
But thoughts denying feeling, every thought
  Some buried feeling's ghost, a spirit pale,
  Sprang up, and wordy nothings could prevail
And juggle with my soul; since, better taught,
The Christian's apprehension, light that solves
  Doubt without logic, rose in logic's room;
Sweet faith came back, sweet faith that hope involves
  And joys, like stars, which, though they not illume
This mortal night, have glory that dissolves
  And strikes to quick transparence all its gloom.

The Army Surgeon

Over that breathing waste of friends and foes,
The wounded and the dying, hour by hour,—
In will a thousand, yet but one in power,—
He labours thro' the red and groaning day.
The fearful moorland where the myriads lay
Moved as a moving field of mangled worms.
And as a raw brood, orphaned in the storms,
Thrust up their heads if the wind bend a spray
Above them, but when the bare branch performs
No sweet parental office, sink away
With hopeless chirp of woe, so as he goes
Around his feet in clamorous agony
They rise and fall; and all the seething plain
Bubbles a cauldron vast of many-coloured pain.

The Common Grave

Last night beneath the foreign stars I stood
And saw the thoughts of those at home go by
To the great grave upon the hill of blood.
Upon the darkness they went visibly,
Each in the vesture of its own distress.
Among them there came One, frail as a sigh,
And like a creature of the wilderness
Dug with her bleeding hands. She neither cried
Nor wept: nor did she see the many stark
And dead that lay unburied at her side.
All night she toiled, and at that time of dawn,
When Day and Night do change their More or Less,
And Day is More, I saw the melting Dark
Stir to the last, and knew she laboured on.

Introductory Sonnet to 'The House of Life'

A Sonnet is a moment's monument,—
Memorial from the Soul's eternity
To one dead deathless hour. Look that it be,
Whether for lustral rite or dire portent,
Or its own arduous fullness reverent:
Carve it in ivory or in ebony
As Day or Night shall rule; and let Time see
Its flowering crest impearled and orient.
A sonnet is a coin: its face reveals
The soul,—its converse, to what Power 'tis due:—
Whether for tribute to the august appeals
Of Life, or dower in Love's high retinue
It serve, or, mid the dark wharf's cavernous breath,
In Charon's palm it pay the toll to Death.

A Superscription

Look in my face; my name is Might-have-been;
I am also called No-more, Too-late, Farewell;
Unto thine ear I hold the dead-sea shell
Cast up thy Life's foam-fretted feet between,
Unto thine eyes the glass where that is seen
Which had Life's form and Love's, but by my spell
Is now a shaken shadow intolerable,
Of ultimate things unuttered the frail screen.
Mark me, how still I am! But should there dart
One moment through thy soul the soft surprise
Of that winged Peace which lulls the breath of sighs,—
Then shalt thou see me smile, and turn apart
Thy visage of mine ambush at thy heart,
Sleepless, with cold commemorative eyes.

Raleigh's Cell in the Tower

Here writ was the World's History by his hand
  Whose steps knew all the earth; albeit his world
  In these few piteous paces then was furled.
Here daily, hourly, have his proud feet spanned
This smaller speck than the receding land
  Had ever shown his ships; what time he hurled
  Abroad o'er new-found regions spiced and pearled
His country's high dominion and command.

Here dwelt two spheres. The vast terrestrial zone
  His spirit traversed; and that spirit was
    Itself the zone celestial, round whose birth
    The planets played within the zodiac's girth;
  Till hence, through unjust death unfeared, did pass
His spirit to the only land unknown.

Lost Days

The lost days of my life until to-day,
  What were they, could I see them on the street
  Lie as they fell? Would they be ears of wheat
Sown once for food, but trodden into clay?
Or golden coins squandered and still to pay?
  Or drops of blood dabbling the guilty feet?
  Or such spilt water as in dreams must cheat
The undying throats of Hell, athirst alway?

I do not see them here; but after death
  God knows I know the faces I shall see,
Each one a murdered self, with low last breath.
  'I am thyself,—what hast though done to me?'
'And I—and I—thyself' (lo! each one saith),
  'And thou thyself to all eternity!'

On the Site of a Mulberry-Tree
Planted by Wm. Shakespeare; felled by the Rev. F. Gastrell

This tree, here fall'n, no common birth or death
Shared with its kind. The world's enfranchised son,
Who found the trees of Life and Knowledge one,
Here set it, frailer than his laurel-wreath.
Shall not the wretch whose hand it fell beneath
Rank also singly—the supreme unhung?
Lo! Sheppard, Turpin, pleading with black tongue
This viler thief's unsuffocated breath!
We'll search thy glossary, Shakespeare! whence almost,
And whence alone, some name shall be reveal'd
For this deaf drudge, to whom no length of ears
Sufficed to catch the music of the spheres;
Whose soul is carrion now,—too mean to yield
Some Starveling's ninth allotment of a ghost.

Dawn on the Night-Journey

Till dawn the wind drove round me. It is past
And still, and leaves the air to lisp of bird,
And to the quiet that is almost heard
Of the new-risen day, as yet bound fast
In the first warmth of sunrise. When the last
Of the sun's hours to-day shall be fulfilled,
There shall another breath of time be stilled
For me, which now is to my senses cast
As much beyond me as eternity,
Unknown, kept secret. On the newborn air
The moth quivers in silence. It is vast,
Yes, even beyond the hills upon the sea,
The day whose end shall give this hour as sheer
As chaos to the irrevocable Past.

Inconclusiveness

The changing guests, each in a different mood,
  Sit at the roadside table and arise:
  And every life among them in likewise
Is a soul's board set daily with new food.
What man has bent o'er his son's sleep, to brood
  How that face shall watch his when cold it lies?
  Or thought, as his own mother kissed his eyes,
Of what her kiss was when his father wooed?

May not this ancient room thou sit'st in dwell
  In separate living souls for joy or pain?
  Nay, all its corners may be painted plain
Where Heaven shows pictures of some life spent well;
  And may be stamped, a memory all in vain,
Upon the sight of lidless eyes in Hell.

Without Her

What of her glass without her? the blank grey
  There where the pool is blind of the moon's face.
  Her dress without her? the tossed empty space
Of cloud-rack whence the moon has passed away.
Her paths without her? Day's appointed sway
  Usurped by desolate night. Her pillowed place
  Without her! Tears, Ah me! for love's good grace
And cold forgetfulness of night or day.

What of the heart without her? Nay, poor heart,
  Of thee what word remains ere speech be still?
  A wayfarer by barren ways and chill,
Steep ways and weary, without her thou art,
Where the long cloud, the long wood's counterpart,
  Sheds doubled darkness up the labouring hill.

Barren Spring

Once more the changed year's turning wheel returns:
  And as a girl sails balanced in the wind,
  And now before and now again behind
Stoops as it swoops, with cheek that laughs and burns,—
So Spring comes merry towards me here, but earns
  No answering smile from me, whose life is twin'd
  With the dead boughs that winter still must bind,
And whom today the Spring no more concerns.

Behold, this crocus is a withering flame;
  This snowdrop, snow; this apple-blossom's part
  To breed the fruit that breeds the serpent's art.
Nay, for these Spring-flowers, turn thy face from them,
Nor stay till on the year's last lily-stem
  The white cup shrivels round the golden heart.

GEORGE MEREDITH

To a Friend recently lost—T.T.

When I remember, Friend, whom lost I call
  Because a man beloved is taken hence,
  The tender humour and the fire of sense
In your good eyes: how full of heart for all,
And chiefly for the weaker by the wall,
  You bore that light of sane benevolence:
  Then see I round you Death his shadows dense
Divide, and at your feet his emblems fall.
For surely are you one with the white host,
  Spirits, whose memory is our vital air,
    Through the great love of earth they had: lo, these,
    Like beams that throw the path on tossing seas,
Can bid us feel we keep them in the ghost,
  Partakers of a strife they joyed to share.

Lucifer in Starlight

On a starred night Prince Lucifer uprose.
Tired of his dark dominion swung the fiend
Above the rolling ball in cloud part screened,
Where sinners hugged their spectre of repose.
Poor prey to his hot fit of pride were those.
And now upon his western wing he leaned,
Now his huge bulk o'er Africa careened,
Now the black planet shadowed Arctic snows.
Soaring through wider zones that pricked his scars
With memory of the old revolt from Awe,
He reached a middle height, and at the stars,
Which are the brain of heaven, he looked, and sank.
Around the ancient track marched, rank on rank,
The army of unalterable law.

CHRISTINA ROSSETTI

Remember

Remember me when I am gone away,
   Gone far away into the silent land;
   When you can no more hold me by the hand,
Nor I half turn to go yet turning stay.
Remember me when no more day by day
   You tell me of our future that you planned:
   Only remember me; you understand
It will be late to counsel then or pray.
Yet if you should forget me for a while
   And afterwards remember, do not grieve:
   For if the darkness and corruption leave
   A vestige of the thoughts that once I had,
Better by far you should forget and smile
   Than that you should remember and be sad.

Rest

O Earth, lie heavily upon her eyes;
  Seal her sweet eyes weary of watching, Earth;
  Lie close around her; leave no room for mirth
With its harsh laughter, nor for sound of sighs.
She hath no questions, she hath no replies,
  Hushed in and curtained with a blessèd dearth
  Of all that irked her from the hour of birth;
With stillness that is almost Paradise.
Darkness more clear than noon-day holdeth her,
  Silence more musical than any song;
Even her very heart has ceased to stir:
Until the morning of Eternity
Her rest shall not begin nor end, but be;
  And when she wakes she will not think it long.

The Thread of Life

The irresponsive silence of the land,
  The irresponsive sounding of the sea,
  Speak both one message of one sense to me:—
Aloof, aloof, we stand aloof, so stand
Thou too aloof bound with the flawless band
  Of inner solitude; we bind not thee;
  But who from thy self-chain shall set thee free?
What heart shall touch thy heart? what hand thy hand?—
And I am sometimes proud and sometimes meek,
  And sometimes I remember days of old
When fellowship seemed not so far to seek
  And all the world and I seemed much less cold,
  And at the rainbow's foot lay surely gold,
And hope felt strong and life itself not weak.

Go from me, summer friends, and tarry not

Go from me, summer friends, and tarry not:
I am no summer friend, but wintry cold.
A silly sheep benighted from the cold,
A sluggard with a thorn-choked garden plot.
Take counsel, sever from my lot your lot,
Dwell in your pleasant places, hoard your gold;
Lest you with me should shiver on the wold,
Athirst and hungering on a barren spot.
For I have hedged me with a thorny hedge,
I live alone, I look to die alone:
Yet sometimes when a wind sighs through the sedge,
Ghosts of my buried years and friends come back;
My heart goes sighing after swallows flown
On sometime summer's unreturning track.

Thus am I mine own prison

Thus am I mine own prison. Everything
Around me free and sunny and at ease:
Or if in shadow, in a shade of trees
Which the sun kisses, where the gay birds sing
And where all winds make virtuous murmuring;
Where bees are found, with honey for the bees;
Where sounds are music, and where silences
Are music of an unlike fashioning.
Then gaze I at the merry-making crew,
And smile a moment and a moment sigh
Thinking: Why cannot I rejoice with you?
But soon I put the foolish fancy by:
I am not what I have nor what I do;
But what I was I am, I am even I.

Something this foggy day

Something this foggy day, a something which
  Is neither of this fog nor of today,
Has set me dreaming of the winds that play
Past certain cliffs, along one certain beach,
  And turn the topmost edge of waves to spray:
  Ah pleasant pebbly strand so far away,
So out of reach while quite within my reach,
  As out of reach as India or Cathay!
I am sick of where I am and where I am not,
  I am sick of foresight and of memory,
I am sick of all I have and all I see,
  I am sick of self, and there is nothing new;
Oh weary impatient patience of my lot!—
  Thus with myself: how fares it, Friends, with you?

JAMES THOMSON (B.V.)

Striving to sing glad songs

Striving to sing glad songs, I but attain
Wild discords sadder than grief's saddest tune,
As if an owl, with his harsh screech, should strain
To overgratulate a thrush of June.
The nightingale upon its thorny spray
Finds inspiration in the sullen dark:
The kindling dawn, the world-wide joyous day,
Are inspiration to the soaring lark.
The seas are silent in the sunny calm;
Their anthem-surges in the tempest boom.
The skies outroll no solemn thunder psalm
Till they have clothed themselves with clouds of gloom.
My mirth can laugh and talk, but cannot sing;
My grief finds harmonies in everything.

Cor Cordium

O heart of hearts, the chalice of love's fire,
Hid round with flowers and all the bounty of bloom;
O wonderful and perfect heart, for whom
The lyrist liberty made life a lyre;
O heavenly heart, at whose most dear desire
Dead love, living and singing, cleft his tomb,
And with him risen and regent in death's room
All day thy choral pulses rang full choir;
O heart whose beating blood was running song,
O sole thing sweeter than thine own songs were,
Help us for thy free love's sake to be free,
True for thy truth's sake, for thy strength's sake strong,
Till very liberty make clean and fair
The nursing earth as the sepulchral sea.

DAVID GRAY

Hew Atlas for my monument

Hew Atlas for my monument: upraise
A pyramid for my tomb, that undestroyed
By rank oblivion and the hungry void,
My name shall echo through prospective days.
O careless conqueror! cold abysmal grave,—
Is it not sad,—is it not sad, my heart—
To smother young ambition, and depart,
Unhonoured and unwilling, like death's slave?
No rare immortal remnant of my thought
Embalms my life; no poem firmly reared
Against the shock of time, ignobly feared,
But all my life's progression come to nought.
Hew Atlas! build a pyramid in a plain!
O cool the fever burning in my brain!

Don Quixote

Behind thy pasteboard, on thy battered hack,
Thy lean cheek striped with plaster to and fro,
Thy long spear levelled at the unseen foe,
And doubtful Sancho trudging at thy back,
Thou wert a figure strange enough, good lack,
To make wiseacredom, both high and low,
Rub purblind eyes, and, having watched thee go,
Dispatch its Dogberrys upon thy track:
Alas, poor Knight! Alas! poor soul possest!
Yet would today, when courtesy grows chill,
And life's fine loyalties are turned to jest,
Some fire of thine might burn within us still!
Ah, would but one might lay his lance in rest,
And charge in earnest,—were it but a mill.

THOMAS HARDY

To the Matterhorn (June–July 1897)

Thirty-two years since, up against the sun,
Seven shapes, thin atomies to lower sight,
Labouringly leapt and gained thy gabled height,
And four lives paid for what the seven had won.

They were the first by whom the deed was done,
And when I look at thee, my mind takes flight
To that day's tragic feat of manly might,
As though, till then, of history thou hadst none.

Yet ages ere men topped thee, late and soon
Thou didst behold the planets lift and lower;
Saw'st, maybe, Joshua's pausing sun and moon,
And the betokening sky when Caesar's power
Approached its bloody end; yea, even that Noon
When darkness filled the earth till the ninth hour.

At a Lunar Eclipse

Thy shadow, Earth, from Pole to Central Sea,
Now steals along upon the Moon's meek shine
In even monochrome and curving line
Of imperturbable serenity.
How shall I link such sun-cast symmetry
With the torn troubled form I know as thine,
That profile, placid as a brow divine,
With continents of moil and misery?
And can immense Mortality but throw
So small a shade, and Heaven's high human scheme
Be hemmed within the coasts yon arc implies?
Is such the stellar gauge of earthly show,
Nation at war with nation, brains that teem,
Heroes, and woman fairer than the skies?

She, to Him

i

When you shall see me in the toils of Time,
My lauded beauties carried off from me,
My eyes no longer stars as in their prime,
My name forgot of Maiden Fair and Free;

When in your being heart concedes to mind,
And judgement, though you scarce its process know,
Recalls the excellences I once enshrined,
And you are irk'd that they have wither'd so;

Remembering mine the loss is, not the blame,
That Sportsman Time but rears his brood to kill,
Knowing me in my soul the very same—
One who would die to spare you touch of ill!—
Will you not grant to old affection's claim
The hand of friendship down Life's sunless hill?

ii

Perhaps, long hence, when I have pass'd away,
Some other's feature, accent, thought like mine,
Will carry you back to what I used to say,
And bring some memory of your love's decline.

Then you may pause awhile and think, 'Poor jade!'
And yield a sigh to me—as ample due,
Not as the tittle of a debt unpaid
To one who could resign her all to you—

And thus reflecting, you will never see
That your thin thought, in two small words convey'd,
Was no such fleeting phantom-thought to me,
But the Whole Life wherein my part was play'd;
And you amid its fitful masquerade
A Thought—as I in yours but seem to be.

A Church Romance

She turned in the high pew, until her sight
Swept the west gallery, and caught its row
Of music-men with viol, book, and bow
Against the sinking sad tower-window light.

She turned again; and in her pride's despite
One strenuous viol's inspirer seemed to throw
A message from his string to her below,
Which said: 'I claim thee as my own forthright!'

Thus their hearts' bond began, in due time signed.
And long years thence, when Age had scared Romance,
At some old attitude of his or glance
That gallery-scene would break upon her mind,
With him as minstrel, ardent, young, and trim,
Bowing 'New Sabbath' or 'Mount Ephraim.'

We are getting to the end

We are getting to the end of visioning
The impossible within this universe,
Such as that better whiles may follow worse,
And that our race may mend by reasoning.

We know that even as larks in cages sing
Unthoughtful of deliverance from the curse
That holds them lifelong in a latticed hearse,
We ply spasmodically our pleasuring.

And that when nations set them to lay waste
Their neighbours' heritage by foot and horse,
And hack their pleasant plains in festering seams,
They may again,—not warely, or from taste,
But tickled mad by some demonic force.—
Yes. We are getting to the end of dreams!

WILFRED SCAWEN BLUNT

St Valentine's Day

Today, all day, I rode upon the down,
With hounds and horsemen, a brave company;
On this side in its glory lay the sea,
On that the Sussex weald, a sea of brown.
The wind was light, and brightly the sun shone,
And still we gallop'd on from gorse to gorse:
And once, when check'd, a thrush sang, and my horse
Prick'd his quick ears as to a sound unknown.
I knew the Spring was come. I knew it even
Better than all by this, that through my chase
In bush and stone and hill and sea and heaven
I seem'd to see and follow still your face.
Your face my quarry was. For it I rode,
My horse a thing of wings, myself a god.

Gibraltar

Seven weeks of sea, and twice seven days of storm
Upon the huge Atlantic, and once more
We ride into still water and the calm
Of a sweet evening, screen'd by either shore
Of Spain and Barbary. Our toils are o'er,
Our exile is accomplish'd. Once again
We look on Europe, mistress as of yore
Of the fair earth and of the hearts of men.
  Ay, this is the famed rock which Hercules
And Goth and Moor bequeath'd us. At this door
England stands sentry. God! to hear the shrill
Sweet treble of her fifes upon the breeze,
And at the summons of the rock gun's roar
To see her red coats marching from the hill!

ANDREW LANG

The Odyssey

As one that for a weary space has lain
  Lull'd by the song of Circe and her wine
  In gardens near the pale of Proserpine,
Where that Ægean isle forgets the main,
And only the low lutes of love complain,
  And only shadows of wan lovers pine—
  As such an one were glad to know the brine
Salt on his lips, and the large air again—
So gladly from the songs of modern speech
  Men turn, and see the stars, and feel the free
  Shrill wind beyond the close of heavy flowers,
  And through the music of the languid hours
They hear like Ocean on a western beach
  The surge and thunder of the Odyssey.

The Windhover
(To Christ our Lord)

I caught this morning morning's minion, king-
  dom of daylight's dauphin, dapple-dawn-drawn Falcon, in
    his riding
  Of the rolling level underneath him steady air, and striding
High there, how he rung upon the rein of a wimpling wing
In his ecstasy! then off, off forth on swing,
  As a skate's heel sweeps smooth on a bow-bend: the hurl
    and gliding
  Rebuffed the big wind. My heart in hiding
Stirred for a bird,—the achieve of, the mastery of the thing!

Brute beauty and valour and act, oh, air, pride, plume, here
  Buckle! AND the fire that breaks from thee then, a billion
Times told lovelier, more dangerous, O my chevalier!

  No wonder of it: shéer plód makes plough down sillion
Shine, and blue-bleak embers, ah my dear,
  Fall, gall themselves, and gash gold-vermilion.

Spring

Nothing is so beautiful as Spring—
  When weeds, in wheels, shoot long and lovely and lush;
  Thrush's eggs look little low heavens, and thrush
Through the echoing timber does so rinse and wring
The ear, it strikes like lightnings to hear him sing;
  The glassy peartree leaves and blooms, they brush
  The descending blue; that blue is all in a rush
With richness; the racing lambs too have fair their fling.

What is all this juice and all this joy?
  A strain of the earth's sweet being in the beginning
    In Eden's garden.—Have, get, before it cloy,

  Before it cloud, Christ, lord, and sour with sinning,
Innocent mind and Mayday in girl and boy,
  Most, O maid's child, thy choice and worthy the winning.

God's Grandeur

The world is charged with the grandeur of God.
  It will flame out, like shining from shook foil;
  It gathers to a greatness, like the ooze of oil
Crushed. Why do men then now not reck his rod?
Generations have trod, have trod, have trod;
  And all is seared with trade; bleared, smeared with toil;
  And wears man's smudge and shares man's smell: the soil
Is bare now, nor can foot feel, being shod.

And for all this, nature is never spent;
  There lives the dearest freshness deep down things;
And though the last lights off the black West went
  Oh, morning, at the brown brink eastward, springs—
Because the Holy Ghost over the bent
  World broods with warm breast and with ah! bright wings.

As kingfishers catch fire

As kingfishers catch fire, dragonflies draw flame;
As tumbled over rim in roundy wells
Stones ring; like each tucked string tells, each hung bell's
Bow swung finds tongue to fling out broad its name;
Each mortal thing does one thing and the same;
Deals out that being indoors each one dwells;
Selves—goes itself; *myself* it speaks and spells,
Crying *What I do is me; for that I came.*

I say more: the just man justices;
Keeps grace: that keeps all his goings graces;
Acts in God's eyes what in God's eye he is—
Christ. For Christ plays in ten thousand places,
Lovely in limbs, and lovely in eyes not his
To the Father through the features of men's faces.

Thou art indeed just, Lord

Thou art indeed just, Lord, if I contend
With thee; but, sir, so what I plead is just.
Why do sinners' ways prosper? and why must
Disappointment all my endeavour end?
Wert thou my enemy, O thou my friend,
How wouldst thou worse, I wonder, than thou dost
Defeat, thwart me? Oh, the sots and thralls of lust
Do in spare hours more thrive than I that spend,
Sir, life upon thy cause. See, banks and brakes
Now, leavéd how thick! lacéd they are again
With fretty chervil, look, and fresh wind shakes
Them; birds build—but not I build; no but strain,
Time's eunuch, and not breed one work that wakes.
Mine, O thou lord of life, send my roots rain.

Not, I'll not, carrion comfort

Not, I'll not, carrion comfort, Despair, not feast on thee;
Not untwist—slack they may be—these last strands of man
In me ór, most weary, cry *I can no more*. I can;
Can something, hope, wish day come, not choose not to be.
But ah, but O thou terrible, why wouldst thou rude on me
Thy wring-world right foot rock? lay a lionlimb against me? scan
With darksome devouring eyes my bruisèd bones? and fan,
O in turns of tempest, me heaped there; me frantic to avoid thee
and flee?

Why? That my chaff might fly; my grain lie, sheer and clear.
Nay in all that toil, that coil, since (seems) I kissed the rod,
Hand rather, my heart lo! lapped strength, stole joy, would laugh,
chéer.
Cheer whom though? the hero whose heaven-handling flung me,
fóot tród
Me? or me that fought him? O which one? is it each one? That
night, that year
Of now done darkness I wretch lay wrestling with (my God!)
my God.

No worst, there is none

No worst, there is none. Pitched past pitch of grief,
More pangs will, schooled at forepangs, wilder wring.
Comforter, where, where is your comforting?
Mary, mother of us, where is your relief?
My cries heave, herds-long; huddle in a main, a chief
Woe, world-sorrow; on an age-old anvil wince and sing—
Then lull, then leave off. Fury had shrieked 'No ling-
ering! Let me be fell: force I must be brief.'

O the mind, mind has mountains; cliffs of fall
Frightful, sheer, no-man-fathomed. Hold them cheap
May who ne'er hung there. Nor does long our small
Durance deal with that steep or deep. Here! creep,
Wretch, under a comfort serves in a whirlwind: all
Life death does end and each day dies with sleep.

Patience

Patience, hard thing! the hard thing but to pray,
But bid for, Patience is! Patience who asks
Wants war, wants wounds; weary his times, his tasks;
To do without, take tosses, and obey.

Rare patience roots in these, and, these away,
Nowhere. Natural heart's ivy, Patience masks
Our ruins of wrecked past purpose. There she basks
Purple eyes and seas of liquid leaves all day.

We hear our hearts grate on themselves: it kills
To bruise them dearer. Yet the rebellious wills
Of us we do bid God bend to him even so.

And where is he who more and more distils
Delicious kindness?—He is patient. Patience fills
His crisp combs, and that comes those ways we know.

O my uncared-for songs

O my uncared-for songs, what are ye worth,
That in my secret book with so much care
I write you, this one here and that one there,
Marking the time and order of your birth?
How, with a fancy so unkind to mirth,
A sense so hard, a style so worn and bare,
Look ye for any welcome anywhere
From any shelf or heart-home on the earth?

Should others ask you this, say then I yearn'd
To write you such as once, when I was young,
Finding I should have loved and thereto turn'd.
'Twere something yet to live again among
The gentle youth beloved, and where I learn'd
My art, be there remember'd for my song.

While yet we wait for spring

While yet we wait for spring, and from the dry
And blackening east that so embitters March,
Well-housed must watch grey fields and meadows parch,
And driven dust and withering snowflake fly;
Already in glimpses of the tarnish'd sky
The sun is warm and beckons to the larch,
And where the covert hazels interarch
Their tassell'd twigs, fair beds of primrose lie.

Beneath the crisp and wintry carpet hid
A million buds but stay their blossoming;
And trustful birds have built their nests amid
The shuddering boughs, and only wait to sing
Till one soft shower from the south shall bid,
And hither tempt the pilgrim steps of spring.

Democritus

Joy of your opulent atoms! wouldst thou dare
Say that Thought also of atoms self-became,
Waving to soul as light had the eye in aim;
And so with things of bodily sense compare
Those native notions that the heavens declare,
Space and Time, Beauty and God—Praise we his name!—
Read ideas, that on tongues of flame
From out mind's cooling paste leapt unaware?

Thy spirit, Democritus, orb'd in the eterne
Illimitable galaxy of night
Shineth undimm'd where greater splendours burn
Of sage and poet: by their influence bright
We are held; and pouring from his quenchless urn
Christ with immortal love-beams laves the height.

ARTHUR O'SHAUGHNESSY

The Line of Beauty

When mountains crumble and rivers all run dry,
When every flower has fallen, and summer fails
To come again, when the sun's splendour pales,
And earth with lagging footsteps seems well-nigh
Spent in her annual circuit through the sky;
When love is a quenched flame, and nought avails
To save decrepit man, who feebly wails,
And lies down lost in the great grave to die,
What is eternal? What escapes decay?
A certain faultless, matchless, deathless line,
Curving consummate. Death, Eternity
Add nought to it, from it take nought away.
'Twas all God's gift, and all man's mastery,
God become human, and man grown divine.

Sunken Gold

In dim green depths rot ingold-laden ships,
While gold doubloons that from the drowned hand fell
Lie nestled in the ocean's flower bell
With Love's gemmed rings once kissed by now dead lips.
And round some wrought-gold cup the sea-grass whips
And hides lost pearls, near pearls still in their shell,
Where seaweed forests fill each ocean dell,
And seek dim sunlight with their countless tips.

So lie the wasted gifts, the long-lost hopes,
Beneath the now hushed surface of myself,
In lonelier depths than where the diver gropes
They lie deep, deep; but I at times behold
In doubtful glimpses, on some reefy shelf,
The gleam of irrecoverable gold.

What the Sonnet is

Fourteen small broider'd berries on the hem
Of Circe's mantle, each of magic gold;
Fourteen of lone Calypso's tears that roll'd
Into the sea, for pearls to come to them;
Fourteen clear signs of omen in the gem
With which Medea human fate foretold;
Fourteen small drops, which Faustus, growing old,
Craved of the Fiend, to water Life's dry stem.

It is the pure white diamond Dante brought
To Beatrice; the sapphire Laura wore
When Petrarch cut it sparkling out of thought;
The ruby Shakespeare hew'd from his heart's core;
The dark deep emerald that Rossetti wrought
For his own soul, to wear for evermore.

Renouncement

I must not think of thee; and, tired yet strong,
  I shun the thought that lurks in all delight—
  The thought of thee—and in the blue Heaven's height,
And in the dearest passage of a song.

Oh, just beyond the fairest thoughts that throng
  This breast, the thought of thee waits hidden, yet bright;
  But it must never, never come in sight;
I must stop short of thee the whole day long.

But when sleep comes to close each difficult day,
  When night gives pause to the long watch I keep,
    And all my bonds I needs must loose apart,
Must doff my will as raiment laid away,—
  With the first dream that comes with the first sleep
    I run, I run, I am gathered to thy heart.

W. E. HENLEY

Apparition

Thin-legged, thin-chested, slight unspeakably,
Neat-footed and weak-fingered: in his face,—
Lean, large-boned, curved of beak, and touched with race,
Bold-lipped, rich-tinted, mutable as the sea,
The brown eyes radiant with vivacity—
There shines a brilliant and romantic grace,
A spirit intense and rare, with trace on trace
Of passion and impudence and energy,
Valiant in velvet, light in rugged luck,
Most vain, most generous, sternly critical,
Buffoon and poet, lover and sensualist,
A deal of Ariel, just a streak of Puck,
Much Antony, of Hamlet most of all,
And something of the Shorter-Catechist.

On the sale by auction of Keats' love letters

These are the letters which Endymion wrote
To one he loved in secret, and apart.
And now the brawlers of the auction mart
Bargain and bid for each poor blotted note,
Ay! for each separate pulse of passion quote
The merchant's price. I think they love not art
Who break the crystal of a poet's heart
That small and sickly eyes may glare and gloat.
Is it not said that many years ago,
In a far Eastern town, some soldiers ran
With torches through the midnight, and began
To wrangle for mean raiment, and to throw
Dice for the garments of a wretched man,
Not knowing the God's wonder, or His woe?

W. B. YEATS

Leda and the Swan

A sudden blow; the great wings beating still
Above the staggering girl, her thighs caressed
By the dark webs, her nape caught in his bill,
He holds her helpless breast upon his breast.

How can those terrified vague fingers push
The feathered glory from her loosening thighs?
And how can body, laid in that white rush,
But feel the strange heart beating where it lies?

A shudder in the loins engenders there
The broken wall, the burning roof and tower
And Agamemnon dead.
Being so caught up,
So mastered by the brute blood of the air,
Did she put on his knowledge with his power
Before the indifferent beak could let her drop?

The Night Nurse goes her Round

Droop under doves' wings silent, breathing shapes
white coverlids dissimulate; in hope
of opiate aid to round the ledge where gapes
the sootblack gulf in which obtuse minds grope

for very nothing, vast and undefined,
in starless depths no astrolabe can probe.
The moving form, as doomed to pass and wind,
unwind and pass anew, in sleep-dyed robe

of firmamental silence more than hue,
watches the doorway of the tired's escape
only. Fatigue goes on; I left behind

with moths' feet, wordless whispering; or find
reality, white coiffe and scarlet cape;
and dreams are what a dream should be, or true.

LIONEL JOHNSON

Bagley Wood

The night is full of stars, full of magnificence:
Nightingales hold the wood, and fragrance loads the dark.
Behold, what fires august, what lights eternal! Hark,
What passionate music poured in passionate love's defence!
Breathe but the wafting wind's nocturnal frankincense!
Only to feel this night's great heart, only to mark
The splendours and the glooms, brings back the patriarch,
Who on Chaldean wastes found God through reverence.
Could we but live at will upon this perfect height,
Could we but always keep the passion of this peace,
Could we but face unshamed the look of this pure light,
Could we but win earth's heart, and give desire release:
Then were we all divine, and then were ours by right
These stars, these nightingales, these scents: then shame
would cease.

Experience

The burden of the long gone years: the weight,
The lifeless weight, of miserable things
Done long ago, not done with: the live stings
Left by old joys, follies provoking fate,
Showing their sad side, when it is too late:
Dread burden, that remorseless knowledge brings
To men, remorseful! But the burden clings:
And that remorse declares that bitter state.

Wisdom of ages! Wisdom of old age!
Written, and spoken of, and prophesied,
The common record of humanity!
Oh, vain! The springtime is our heritage
First, and the sunlight on the flowing tide:
Then, that old truth's confirming misery.

ERNEST DOWSON

A Last Word

Let us go hence: the night is now at hand;
The day is overworn, the birds all flown;
And we have reaped the crops the gods have sown;
Despair and death; deep darkness o'er the land,
Broods like an owl; we cannot understand
Laughter or tears, for we have only known
Surpassing vanity: vain things alone
Have driven our perverse and aimless band.
Let us go hence, somewhither strange and cold,
To Hollow Lands where just men and unjust
Find end of labour, where's rest for the old,
Freedom to all from love and fear and lust.
Twine our torn hands! O pray the earth enfold
Our life-sick hearts and turn them into dust.

George Crabbe

Give him the darkest inch your shelf allows,
Hide him in lonely garrets, if you will,—
But his hard, human pulse is throbbing still
With the sure strength that fearless truth endows.
In spite of all fine science disavows,
Of his plain excellence and stubborn skill
There yet remains what fashion cannot kill,
Though years have thinned the laurel from his brows.

Whether or not we read him, we can feel
From time to time the vigor of his name
Against us like a finger for the shame
And emptiness of what our souls reveal
In books that are as altars where we kneel
To consecrate the flicker, not the flame.

Charles Carville's Eyes

A melancholy face Charles Carville had,
But not so melancholy as it seemed,
When once you knew him, for his mouth redeemed
His insufficient eyes, forever sad:
In them there was no life-glimpse, good or bad,
Nor joy nor passion in them ever gleamed;
His mouth was all of him that ever beamed,
His eyes were sorry, but his mouth was glad.

He never was a fellow that said much,
And half of what he did say was not heard
By many of us: we were out of touch
With all his whims and all his theories
Till he was dead, so those blank eyes of his
Might speak them. Then we heard them, every word.

Many Are Called

The Lord Apollo, who has never died,
Still holds alone his immemorial reign,
Supreme in an impregnable domain
That with his magic he has fortified;
And though melodious multitudes have tried
In ecstasy, in anguish, and in vain,
With invocation sacred and profane
To lure him, even the loudest are outside.

Only at unconjectured intervals,
By will of him on whom no man may gaze,
By word of him whose law no man has read,
A questing light may rift the sullen walls,
To cling where mostly its infrequent rays
Fall golden on the patience of the dead.

The Sheaves

Where long the shadows of the wind had rolled,
Green wheat was yielding to the change assigned,
And as by some vast magic undivined
The world was turning slowly into gold.
Like nothing that was ever bought or sold
It waited there, the body and the mind;
And with a mighty meaning of a kind
That tells the more the more it is not told.

So in a land where all days are not fair,
Fair days went on till on another day
A thousand golden sheaves were lying there,
Shining and still, but not for long to stay—
As if a thousand girls with golden hair
Might rise from where they slept and go away.

New England

Here where the wind is always north-north-east
And children learn to walk on frozen toes,
Wonder begets an envy of all those
Who boil elsewhere with such a lyric yeast
Of love that you will hear them at a feast
Where demons would appeal for some repose,
Still clamoring where the chalice overflows
And crying wildest who have drunk the least.

Passion is here a soilure of the wits,
We're told, and Love a cross for them to bear;
Joy shivers in the corner where she knits
And Conscience always has the rocking-chair,
Cheerful as when she tortured into fits
The first cat that was ever killed by Care.

Credo

I cannot find my way: there is no star
In all the shrouded heavens anywhere;
And there is not a whisper in the air
Of any living voice but one so far
That I can hear it only as a bar
Of lost, imperial music, played when fair
And angel fingers wove, and unaware,
Dead leaves to garlands where no roses are.

No, there is not a glimmer, nor a call,
For one that welcomes, welcomes when he fears,
The black and awful chaos of the night;
For through it all—above, beyond it all—
I know the far-sent message of the years,
I feel the coming glory of the Light.

In the Dock

Pallid, mis-shapen he stands. The World's grimed thumb,
Now hooked securely in his matted hair,
Has haled him struggling from his poisonous slum
And flung him, mute as fish, close-netted there.

His bloodless hands entalon that iron rail.
He gloats in beastlike trance. His settling eyes
From staring face to face rove on—and quail.
Justice for carrion pants; and these the flies.

Voice after voice in smooth impartial drone
Erects horrific in his darkening brain
A timber framework, where agape, alone,
Bright life will kiss good-bye the cheek of Cain.

Sudden like wolf he cries; and sweats to see
When howls man's soul, it howls inaudibly.

TRUMBULL STICKNEY

Be still. The Hanging Gardens were a dream

Be still. The Hanging Gardens were a dream
That over Persian roses flew to kiss
The curled lashes of Semiramis.
Troy never was, nor green Skamander stream.
Provence and Troubadour are merest lies,
The glorious hair of Venice was a beam
Made with Titian's eye. The sunsets seem,
The world is very old and nothing is.
Be still. Thou foolish thing, thou canst not wake,
Nor thy tears wedge thy soldered lids apart,
But patter in the darkness of thy heart.
Thy brain is plagued. Thou art a frightened owl
Blind with the light of life thou'ldst not forsake,
And error loves and nourishes thy soul.

On some Shells found Inland

These are my murmur-laden shells that keep
A fresh voice tho' the years be very gray.
The wave that washed their lips and tuned their lay
Is gone, gone with the faded ocean sweep,
The royal tide, gray ebb and sunken neap
And purple midday,—gone! To this hot clay
Must sing my shells, where yet the primal day,
Its roar and rhythm and splendour will not sleep.
What hand shall join them to their proper sea
If all be gone? Shall they forever feel
Glories undone and worlds that cannot be?—
'T were mercy to stamp out this agèd wrong,
Dash them to earth and crunch them with the heel
And make a dust of their seraphic song.

The Melancholy Year

The melancholy year is dead with rain.
Drop after drop on every branch pursues.
From far away beyond the drizzled flues
A twilight saddens to the window pane.
And dimly thro' the chambers of the brain,
From place to place and gently touching, moves
My one and irrecoverable love's
Dear and lost shape one other time again.
So in the last of autumn for a day
Summer or summer's memory returns.
So in a mountain desolation burns
Some rich belated flower, and with the gray
Sick weather, in the world of rotting ferns
From out the dreadful stones it dies away.

Six O'Clock

Now burst above the city's cold twilight
The piercing whistles and the tower-clocks:
For day is done. Along the frozen docks
The workmen set their ragged shirts aright.
Thro' factory doors a stream of dingy light
Follows the scrimmage as it quickly flocks
To hut and home among the snow's gray blocks.—
I love you, human labourers. Good-night!
Good-night to all the blackened arms that ache!
Good-night to every sick and sweated brow,
To the poor girl that strength and love forsake,
To the poor boy who can no more! I vow
The victim soon shall shudder at the stake
And fall in blood: we bring him even now.

ROBERT FROST

Mowing

There was never a sound beside the wood but one,
And that was my long scythe whispering to the ground.
What was it it whispered? I knew not well myself;
Perhaps it was something about the heat of the sun,
Something, perhaps, about the lack of sound—
And that was why it whispered and did not speak.
It was no dream of the gift of idle hours,
Or easy gold at the hand of fay or elf:
Anything more than the truth would have seemed too weak
To the earnest love that laid the swale in rows,
Not without feeble-pointed spikes of flowers
(Pale orchises), and scared a bright green snake.
The fact is the sweetest dream that labor knows.
My long scythe whispered and left the hay to make.

Meeting and Passing

As I went down the hill along the wall
There was a gate I had leaned at for the view
And had just turned from when I first saw you
As you came up the hill. We met. But all
We did that day was mingle great and small
Footprints in summer dust as if we drew
The figure of our being less than two
But more than one as yet. Your parasol
Pointed the decimal off with one deep thrust.
And all the time we talked you seemed to see
Something down there to smile at in the dust.
(Oh, it was without prejudice to me!)
Afterward I went past what you had passed
Before we met and you what I had passed.

The Oven Bird

There is a singer everyone has heard,
Loud, a mid-summer and a mid-wood bird,
Who makes the solid tree trunks sound again.
He says that leaves are old and that for flowers
Mid-summer is to spring as one to ten.
He says the early petal-fall is past,
When pear and cherry bloom went down in showers
On sunny days a moment overcast;
And comes that other fall we name the fall.
He says that highway dust is over all.
The bird would cease and be as other birds
But that he knows in singing not to sing.
The question that he frames in all but words
Is what to make of a diminished thing.

Design

I found a dimpled spider, fat and white,
On a white heal-all, holding up a moth
Like a white piece of rigid satin cloth—
Assorted characters of death and blight
Mixed ready to begin the morning right,
Like the ingredients of a witches' broth—
A snow-drop spider, a flower like froth,
And dead wings carried like a paper kite.

What had that flower to do with being white,
The wayside blue and innocent heal-all?
What brought the kindred spider to that height,
Then steered the white moth thither in the night?
What but design of darkness to appall?—
If design govern in a thing so small.

The Silken Tent

She is as in a field a silken tent
At midday when a sunny summer breeze
Has dried the dew and all its ropes relent,
So that in guys it gently sways at ease,
And its supporting central cedar pole,
That is its pinnacle to heavenward
And signifies the sureness of the soul,
Seems to owe naught to any single cord,
But strictly held by none, is loosely bound
By countless silken ties of love and thought
To everything on earth the compass round,
And only by one's going slightly taut
In the capriciousness of summer air
Is of the slightest bondage made aware.

Never Again Would Birds' Song Be The Same

He would declare and could himself believe
That the birds there in all the garden round
From having heard the daylong voice of Eve
Had added to their own an oversound,
Her tone of meaning but without the words.
Admittedly an eloquence so soft
Could only have had an influence on birds
When call or laughter carried it aloft.
Be that as may be, she was in their song.
Moreover her voice upon their voices crossed
Had now persisted in the woods so long
That probably it never would be lost.
Never again would birds' song be the same.
And to do that to birds was why she came.

JOHN MASEFIELD

The Pathfinder (extract)

She lies at grace, at anchor, head to tide,
The wind blows by in vain: she lets it be.
Gurgles of water run along her side,
She does not heed them: they are not the sea.
She is at peace from all her wandering now,
Quiet is in the very bones of her:
The glad thrust of the leaning of her bow
Blows bubbles from the ebb but does not stir.

Rust stains her side, her sails are furled, the smoke
Streams from her galley funnel and is gone;
A gull is settled on her skysail truck.
Some dingy seamen, by her deckhouse, joke;
The river loiters by her with its muck,
And takes her image as a benison.

February Afternoon

Men heard this roar of parleying starlings, saw
A thousand years ago even as now,
Black rooks with white gulls following the plough
So that the first are last until a caw
Commands that last are first again,—a law
Which was of old when one, like me, dreamed how
A thousand years might dust lie on his brow
Yet thus would birds do between hedge and shore.

Time swims before me, making as a day
A thousand years, while the broad ploughland oak
Roars mill-like and men strike and bear the stroke
Of war as ever, audacious or resigned,
And God sits still aloft in the array
That we have wrought him, stone-deaf and stone-blind.

That Girl's Clear Eyes

That girl's clear eyes utterly concealed all
Except that there was something to reveal.
And what did mine say in the interval?
No more; no less. They are but as a seal
Not to be broken till after I am dead;
And then vainly. Everyone of us
This morning at our tasks left nothing said,
In spite of many words. We were sealed thus,
Like tombs. Nor until now could I admit
That all I cared for was the pleasure and pain
I tasted in the stony square sunlit,
Or the dark cloisters, or shade of airy plane,
While music blazed and children, line after line,
Marched past, hiding the "SEVENTEEN THIRTY-NINE."

It Was Upon

It was upon a July evening.
At a stile I stood, looking along a path
Over the country by a second Spring
Drenched perfect green again. "The lattermath
Will be a fine one." So the stranger said,
A wandering man. Albeit I stood at rest,
Flushed with desire I was. The earth outspread,
Like meadows of the future, I possessed.

And as an unaccomplished prophecy
The stranger's words, after the interval
Of a score years, when those fields are by me
Never to be recrossed, now I recall,
This July eve, and question, wondering,
What of the lattermath to his hoar Spring?

Some Eyes Condemn

Some eyes condemn the earth they gaze upon:
Some wait patiently till they know far more
Than earth can tell them: some laugh at the whole
As folly of another's making: one
I knew that laughed because he saw, from core
To rind not one thing worth the laugh his soul
Had ready at waking: some eyes have begun
With laughing; some stand startled at the door.

Others, too, I have seen rest, question, roll,
Dance, shoot. And many I have loved watching. Some
I could not take my eyes from till they turned
And loving died. I had not found my goal.
But thinking of your eyes, dear, I become
Dumb: for they flamed and it was me they burned.

Wild Peaches

1

When the world turns completely upside down
You say we'll emigrate to the Eastern Shore
Aboard a river-boat from Baltimore;
We'll live among wild peach trees, miles from town,
You'll wear a coonskin cap, and I a gown
Homespun, dyed butternut's dark gold colour.
Lost, like your lotus-eating ancestor,
We'll swim in milk and honey till we drown.

The winter will be short, the summer long,
The autumn amber-hued, sunny and hot,
Tasting of cider and of scuppernong;
All seasons sweet, but autumn best of all.
The squirrels in their silver fur will fall
Like falling leaves, like fruit, before your shot.

2

The autumn frosts will lie upon the grass
Like bloom on grapes of purple-brown and gold.
The misted early mornings will be cold;
The little puddles will be roofed with glass.
The sun, which burns from copper into brass,
Melts these at noon, and makes the boys unfold
Their knitted mufflers; full as they can hold,
Fat pockets dribble chestnuts as they pass.

Peaches grow wild, and pigs can live in clover;
A barrel of salted herrings lasts a year;
The spring begins before the winter's over.
By February you may find the skins
Of garter snakes and water moccasins
Dwindled and harsh, dead-white and cloudy-clear.

Chi è questa
(after Cavalcanti)

Who is she that comes, makying turn every man's eye
And makying the air to tremble with a bright clearenesse
That leadeth with her Love, in such nearness
No man may proffer of speech more than a sigh?

Ah God, what she is like when her owne eye turneth, is
Fit for Amor to speake, for I can not at all;
Such is her modesty, I would call
Every woman else but an useless uneasiness.

No one could ever tell all of her pleasauntness
In that every high noble vertu leaneth to herward,
So Beauty sheweth her forth as her Godhede;

Never before was our mind so high led,
Nor have we so much of heal as will afford
That our thought may take her immediate in its embrace.

La bella donna, dove Amor si mostra
(after Cavalcanti)

This fayre Mistress, whereby Love maketh plain
How full he is of prowesse, adornèd to a marvel,
Tuggeth the heart out of thy masking-shell,
The which enhaunceth his life in her domain.

For her quadrangle is guarded with such a sweet smell
Every unicorn of India smelleth it out,
But her virtue against thee in jousting-bout
Turneth against us for to be cruel.

She is, certes, of such great avail
Nothing of all perfectness in her lacketh
That can be in creature subject to death,

Neither in this mortality did foresight fail.
'Tis fitting thy wit known
Only that which it can take, or mistake, for its own.

Voi, che per gli occhi miei passaste al core
(after Cavalcanti)

You, who do breech mine eyes and touch the heart,
And start the mind from her brief reveries,
Might pluck my life and agony apart,
Saw you how love assaileth her with sighs,

And lays about him with so brute a might
That all my wounded senses turn to flight.
There's a new face upon the seigniory,
And new is the voice that maketh loud my grief.

Love, who hath drawn me down through devious ways,
Hath from your noble eyes so swiftly come!
'Tis he hath hurled the dart, wherefrom my pain,

First shot's resultant! and in flanked amaze
See how my affrighted soul recoileth from
That sinister side wherein the heart lies slain.

A me stesso di me gran pietà viene
(after Cavalcanti)

I am reduced at last to self compassion,
For the sore anguish that I see me in;
At my great weakness; that my soul hath been
Concealed beneath her wounds in such a fashion:

Such mine oppression that I know, in brief,
That to my life ill's worst starred ills befall;
And this strange lady on whose grace I call
Maintains continuous my stour of grief,

For when I look in her direction,
She turns upon me her disdeigning eyen
So harshly that my waiting heart is rent
And all my powers and properties are spent,
Till that heart lieth for a sign ill-seen,
Where Amor's cruelty hath hurled him down.

Se merce fosse amica a' miei desiri
(after Cavalcanti)

If Mercy were the friend of my desires,
Or Mercy's source of movement were the heart,
Then, by this fair, would Mercy show such art
And power of healing as my pain requires.

From torturing delight my sighs commence,
Born of the mind where Love is situate,
Go errant forth and naught save grief relate
And find no one to give them audience.

They would return to the eyes in galliard mode,
With all harsh tears and their deep bitterness
Transmuted into revelry and joy;

Were't not unto the sad heart such annoy,
And to the mournful soul such rathe distress
That none doth deign salute them on the road.

A Virginal

No, no! Go from me. I have left her lately.
I will not spoil my sheath with lesser brightness,
For my surrounding air hath a new lightness;
Slight are her arms, yet they have bound me straitly
And left me cloaked as with a gauze of ether;
As with sweet leaves; as with subtle clearness.
Oh, I have picked up magic in her nearness
To sheathe me half in half the things that sheathe her.
No, no! Go from me. I have still the flavour,
Soft as spring wind that's come from birchen bowers.
Green come the shoots, aye April in the branches,
As winter's wound with her sleight hand she staunches,
Hath of the trees a likeness of the savour:
As white their bark, so white this lady's hours.

Still-Life

Through the open French window the warm sun
lights up the polished breakfast-table, laid
round a bowl of crimson roses, for one—
a service of Worcester porcelain, arrayed
near it a melon, peaches, figs, small hot
rolls in a napkin, fairy rack of toast,
butter in ice, high silver coffee-pot,
and, heaped on a salver, the morning's post.

She comes over the lawn, the young heiress,
from her early walk in her garden-wood
feeling that life's a table set to bless
her delicate desires with all that's good,

that even the unopened future lies
like a love-letter, full of sweet surprise.

RUPERT BROOKE

The Soldier

If I should die, think only this of me:
  That there's some corner of a foreign field
That is for ever England. There shall be
  In that rich earth a richer dust conceal'd;
A dust whom England bore, shaped, made aware,
  Gave, once, her flowers to love, her ways to roam,
A body of England's, breathing English air,
  Wash'd by the rivers, blest by suns of home.
And think, this heart, all evil shed away,
  A pulse in the eternal mind, no less
    Gives somewhere back the thoughts by England given;
Her sights and sounds; dreams happy as her day;
  And laughter, learnt of friends; and gentleness,
    In hearts at peace, under an English heaven.

Clouds

Down the blue night the unending columns press
In noiseless tumult, break and wave and flow,
Now tread the far South, or lift rounds of snow
Up to the white moon's hidden loveliness.
Some pause in their grave wandering comradeless,
And turn with profound gesture vague and slow,
As who would pray good for the world, but know
Their benediction empty as they bless.

They say that the Dead die not, but remain
Near to the rich heirs of their grief and mirth.
I think they ride the calm mid-heaven, as these,
In wise majestic melancholy train,
And watch the moon, and the still-raging seas,
And men, coming and going on the earth.

EDWIN MUIR

The Transmutation

That all should change to ghost and glance and gleam,
And so transmuted stand beyond all change,
And we be poised between the unmoving dream
And the sole moving moment—this is strange

Past all contrivance, word, or image, or sound,
Or silence, to express, that we who fall
Through time's long ruin should weave this phantom ground
And in its ghostly borders gather all.

There incorruptible the child plays still,
The lover waits beside the trysting tree,
The good hour spans its heaven, and the ill,
Rapt in their silent immortality,

As in commemoration of a day
That having been can never pass away.

Milton

Milton, his face set fair for Paradise,
And knowing that he and Paradise were lost
In separate desolation, bravely crossed
Into his second night and paid his price.
There towards the end he to the dark tower came
Set square in the gate, a mass of blackened stone
Crowned with vermilion fiends like streamers blown
From a great funnel filled with roaring flame.

Shut in his darkness, these he could not see,
But heard the steely clamour known too well
On Saturday nights in every street in Hell.
Where, past the devilish din, could Paradise be?
A footstep more, and his unblinded eyes
Saw far and near the fields of Paradise.

JOHN CROWE RANSOM

Piazza Piece

—I am a gentleman in a dustcoat trying
To make you hear. Your ears are soft and small
And listen to an old man not at all,
They want the young men's whispering and sighing.
But see the roses on your trellis dying
And hear the spectral singing of the moon;
For I must have my lovely lady soon,
I am a gentleman in a dustcoat trying.

—I am a lady young in beauty waiting
Until my truelove comes, and then we kiss.
But what grey man among the vines is this
Whose words are dry and faint as in a dream?
Back from my trellis, Sir, before I scream!
I am a lady young in beauty waiting.

The End of the World

Quite unexpectedly as Vasserot
The armless ambidextrian was lighting
A match between his great and second toe
And Ralph the lion was engaged in biting
The neck of Madame Sossman while the drum
Pointed, and Teeny was about to cough
In waltz-time swinging Jocko by the thumb—
Quite unexpectedly the top blew off:
And there, there overhead, there, there, hung over
Those thousands of white faces, those dazed eyes,
There in the starless dark the poise, the hover
There with vast wings across the cancelled skies,
There in the sudden blackness the black pall
Of nothing, nothing, nothing—nothing at all.

HUGH MACDIARMID

They Know Not What They Do

Burns in Elysium once every year
Ceases from intercourse and turns aside
Shorn for a day of all his rightful pride,
Wounded by those whom yet he holds most dear.
Chaucer he leaves, and Marlowe, and Shakespeare,
Milton and Wordsworth—and he turns to hide
His privy shame that will not be denied,
And pay his annual penalty of fear.

But Christ comes to him there and takes his arm.
'My followers too,' He says, 'are false as thine,
True to themselves, and ignorant of Me,
Grieve not thy fame seems so compact of harm;
Star of the Sot, Staff of the Philistine
—Truth goes from Calvary to Calvary!'

WILFRED OWEN

Anthem for Doomed Youth

What passing-bells for these who die as cattle?
  Only the monstrous anger of the guns.
Only the stuttering rifles' rapid rattle
Can patter out their hasty orisons.
No mockeries for them from prayers or bells,
  Nor any voice of mourning save the choirs,—
The shrill, demented choirs of wailing shells;
  And bugles calling for them from sad shires.

What candles may be held to speed them all?
  Not in the hands of boys, but in their eyes
Shall shine the holy glimmers of good-byes.
  The pallor of girls' brows shall be their pall;
Their flowers the tenderness of silent minds,
And each slow dusk a drawing-down of blinds.

E. E. CUMMINGS

the Cambridge ladies

the Cambridge ladies who live in furnished souls
are unbeautiful and have comfortable minds
(also, with the church's protestant blessings
daughters, unscented shapeless spirited)
they believe in Christ and Longfellow, both dead,
are invariably interested in so many things—
at the present writing one still finds
delighted fingers knitting for the is it Poles?
perhaps. While permanent faces coyly bandy
scandal of Mrs N and Professor D
. . . . the Cambridge ladies do not care, above
Cambridge if sometimes in its box of
sky lavender and cornerless, the
moon rattles like a fragment of angry candy

next to of course god

'next to of course god america i
love you land of the pilgrims' and so forth oh
say can you see by the dawn's early my
country 'tis of centuries come and go
and are no more what of it we should worry
in every language even deafanddumb
thy sons acclaim your glorious name by gorry
by jingo by gee by gosh by gum
why talk of beauty what could be more beautiful than these heroic happy dead
who rushed like lions to the roaring slaughter
they did not stop to think they died instead
then shall the voice of liberty be mute?'

He spoke. And drank rapidly a glass of water

it is at moments after i have dreamed

it is at moments after i have dreamed
of the rare entertainment of your eyes,
when (being fool to fancy) i have deemed

with your peculiar mouth my heart made wise;
at moments when the glassy darkness holds

the genuine apparition of your smile
(it was through tears always) and silence moulds
such strangeness as was mine a little while;

moments when my once more illustrious arms
are filled with fascination, when my breast
wears the intolerant brightness of your charms:

one pierced moment whiter than the rest

—turning from the tremendous lie of sleep
i watch the roses of the day grow deep.

The Troll's Nosegay

A simple nosegay! was that much to ask?
(Winter still nagged, with scarce a bud yet showing.)
He loved her ill, if he resigned the task.
'Somewhere,' she cried, 'there must be blossom blowing.'
It seems my lady wept and the troll swore
By Heaven he hated tears: he'd cure her spleen—
Where she had begged one flower he'd shower fourscore,
A bunch fit to amaze a China Queen.

Cold fog-drawn Lily, pale mist-magic Rose
He conjured, and in a glassy cauldron set
With elvish unsubstantial Mignonette
And such vague bloom as wandering dreams enclose.
But she?
Awed,
Charmed to tears,
Distracted,
Yet—
Even yet, perhaps, a trifle piqued—who knows?

War and Peace

In sodden trenches I have heard men speak,
though numb and wretched, wise and witty things;
and loved them for the stubbornness that clings
longest to laughter when Death's pulleys creak;

and seeing cool nurses move on tireless feet
to do abominable things with grace,
dreamed them sweet sisters in that haunted place
where with child voices strong men howl or bleat.

Yet now these men lay stubborn courage by,
riding dull-eyed and silent in the train
to old men's stools; or sell gay-coloured socks
and listen fearfully for Death; so I
love the low-laughing girls, who now again
go daintily, in thin and flowery frocks.

ALLEN TATE

Sonnets at Christmas

I

This is the day His hour of life draws near,
Let me get ready from head to foot for it
Most handily with eyes to pick the year
For small feed to reward a feathered wit.
Some men would see it an epiphany
At ease, at food and drink, others at chase
Yet I, stung lassitude, with ecstasy
Unspent argue the season's difficult case
So: Man, dull critter of enormous head,
What would he look at in the coiling sky?
But I must kneel again unto the Dead
While Christmas bells of paper white and red,
Figured with boys and girls spilt from a sled,
Ring out the silence I am nourished by.

2

Ah, Christ, I love you rings to the wild sky
And I must think a little of the past:
When I was ten I told a stinking lie
That got a black boy whipped; but now at last
The going years, caught in an accurate glow,
Reverse like balls englished upon green baize—
Let them return, let the round trumpets blow
The ancient crackle of the Christ's deep gaze.
Deafened and blind, with senses yet unfound,
Am I, untutored to the after-wit
Of knowledge, knowing a nightmare has no sound;
Therefore with idle hands and head I sit
In late December before the fire's daze
Punished by crimes of which I would be quit.

YVOR WINTERS

The Realization

Death. Nothing is simpler. One is dead.
The set face now will fade out; the bare fact,
Related movement, regular, intact,
Is reabsorbed, the clay is on the bed.
The soul is mortal, nothing: the dim head
On the dim pillow, less. But thought clings flat
To this, since it can never follow that
Where no precision of the mind is bred.

Nothing to think of between you and All!
Screaming processionals of infinite
Logic are grinding down receding cold!
O fool! Madness again! Turn not, for it
Lurks in each paintless cranny, and you sprawl
Blurring a definition. Quick! you are old.

The Castle of Thorns

Through autumn evening, water whirls thin blue
From iron to iron pail—old, lined, and pure;
Beneath, the iron is indistinct, secure
In revery that cannot reach to you.
Water it was that always lay between
The mind of men and that harsh wall of thorn,
Of stone impenetrable, where the horn
Hung like the key to what it all might mean.

My goats step guardedly, with delicate
Hard flanks and forest hair, unchanged and firm,
A strong tradition that has not grown old.
Peace to the lips that bend in intricate
Old motions, that flinch not before their term!
Peace to the heart that can accept this cold!

Sonnet to the moon

Now every leaf, though colorless, burns bright
With disembodied and celestial light,
And drops without a movement or a sound
A pillar of darkness to the shifting ground.

The lucent, thin, and alcoholic flame
Runs in the stubble with a nervous aim,
But, when the eye pursues, will point with fire
Each single stubble-tip and strain no higher.

O triple goddess! Contemplate my plight!
Opacity, my fate! Change, my delight!
The yellow tom-cat, sunk in shifting fur,
Changes and dreams, a phosphorescent blur.

Sullen I wait, but still the vision shun.
Bodiless thoughts and thoughtless bodies run.

Apollo and Daphne

Deep in the leafy fierceness of the wood,
Sunlight, the cellular and creeping pyre,
Increased more slowly than aetherial fire:
But it increased and touched her where she stood.
The god had seized her, but the powers of good
Struck deep into her veins; with rending flesh
She fled all ways into the grasses' mesh
And burned more quickly than the sunlight could.
And all her heart broke stiff in leafy flame
That neither rose nor fell, but stood aghast;
And she, rooted in Time's slow agony,
Stirred dully, hard-edged laurel, in the past;
And, like a cloud of silence or a name,
The god withdrew into Eternity.

ROY CAMPBELL

Luis De Camoes

Camoes, alone, of all the lyric race,
Born in the angry morning of disaster,
Can look a common soldier in the face:
I find a comrade where I sought a master:
For daily, while the stinking crocodiles
Glide from the mangroves on the swampy shore,
He shares my awning on the dhow, he smiles,
And tells me that he lived it all before.
Through fire and shipwreck, pestilence and loss,
Led by the ignis fatuus of duty
To a dog's death—yet of his sorrows king—
He shouldered high his voluntary Cross,
Wrestled his hardships into forms of beauty,
And taught his gorgon destinies to sing.

Fight With A Water-Spirit

Though many men had passed the ford, not one
Had ever seen that jeering water-ghost
Denying their true conquest of the stream.
But I, who saw him smile behind a stone,
Stopped, challenged him to justify his boast.
Then came the fight, exhausting as a dream,
With stuff not quite impalpable. He sank,
Sighing, at last, in a small shrinking pile.
But my victorious paean changed to fright
To see once more the pale curve of his flank
There in the water, and his endless smile
Broaden behind the stone. No use to fight.
Better to give the place a holy name,
Go on with less ambition than I came.

Now Let Me Roll

Now let me roll beneath the hooves of chance,
Though they may smash my members, heart or brain.
Worms live when severed—somewhere in the expanse
Of this long body dear life will remain:
Rather than lunge upright amongst the herd,
A face thrust up between the brutish backs,
Staring and yellow, desperate, absurd—
The brief last stand of *homo contumax*.

Life, the proud slattern, blandly will abide
Even in a prone or lacerated host;
But ridicule breaks in upon her pride,
With which she warms her lodging like a frost.
Then she, who any worm or pulp can cherish,
Amid that death of pride herself will perish.

Primrose

Upon a bank I sat, a child made seer
Of one small primrose flowering in my mind.
Better than wealth it is, said I, to find
One small page of Truth's manuscript made clear.
I looked at Christ transfigured without fear—
The light was very beautiful and kind,
And where the Holy Ghost in flame had signed
I read it through the lenses of a tear.
And then my sight grew dim, I could not see
The primrose that had lighted me to Heaven,
And there was but the shadow of a tree
Ghostly among the stars. The years that pass
Like tired soldiers nevermore have given
Moments to see wonders in the grass.

Canal Bank Walk

Leafy-with-love banks and the green waters of the canal
Pouring redemption for me, that I do
The will of God, wallow in the habitual, the banal,
Grow with nature again as before I grew.
The bright stick trapped, the breeze adding a third
Party to the couple kissing on an old seat,
And a bird gathering materials for the nest for the Word
Eloquently new and abandoned to its delirious beat.
O unworn world enrapture me, encapture me in a web
Of fabulous grass and eternal voices by a beech,
Feed the gaping need of my senses, give me ad lib
To pray unselfconsciously with overflowing speech
For this soul needs to be honoured with a new dress woven
From green and blue things and arguments that cannot be proven.

Lines Written On a Seat On the Grand Canal, Dublin

"Erected to the Memory of Mrs Dermot O'Brien"

O commemorate me where there is water,
Canal water preferably, so stilly
Greeny at the heart of summer. Brother
Commemorate me thus beautifully.
Where by a lock niagarously roars
The falls for those who sit in the tremendous silence
Of mid-July. No one will speak in prose
Who finds his way to these Parnassian islands.
A swan goes by head low with many apologies,
Fantastic light looks through the eyes of bridges—
And look! a barge comes bringing from Athy
And other far-flung towns mythologies.
O commemorate me with no hero-courageous
Tomb—just a canal-bank seat for the passer-by.

Epic

I have lived in important places, times
When great events were decided: who owned
That half a rood of rock, a no-man's land
Surrounded by our pitchfork-armed claims.
I heard the Duffys shouting "Damn your soul"
And old McCabe stripped to the waist, seen
Step the plot defying blue cast-steel—
"Here is the march along these iron stones"
That was the year of the Munich bother. Which
Was most important? I inclined
To lose my faith in Ballyrush and Gortin
Till Homer's ghost came whispering to my mind
He said: I made the Iliad from such
A local row. Gods make their own importance.

The Hospital

A year ago I fell in love with the functional ward
Of a chest hospital: square cubicles in a row
Plain concrete, wash basins—an art lover's woe,
Not counting how the fellow in the next bed snored.
But nothing whatever is by love debarred,
The common and banal her heat can know.
The corridor led to a stairway and below
Was the inexhaustible adventure of a gravelled yard.

This is what love does to things: the Rialto Bridge,
The main gate that was bent by a heavy lorry,
The seat at the back of a shed that was a suntrap.
Naming these things is the love-act and its pledge;
For we must record love's mystery without claptrap,
Snatch out of time the passionate transitory.

WILLIAM EMPSON

Camping Out

And now she cleans her teeth into the lake:
Gives it (God's grace) for her own bounty's sake
What morning's pale and the crisp mist debars:
Its glass of the divine (that Will could break)
Restores, beyond Nature: or lets Heaven take
(Itself being dimmed) her pattern, who half awake
Milks between rocks a straddled sky of stars.

Soap tension the star pattern magnifies.
Smoothly Madonna through-assumes the skies
Whose vaults are opened to achieve the Lord.
No, it is we soaring explore galaxies,
Our bullet boat light's speed by thousands flies.
Who moves so among stars their frame unties;
See where they blur, and die, and are outsoared.

Who's Who

A shilling life will give you all the facts:
How Father beat him, how he ran away,
What were the struggles of his youth, what acts
Made him the greatest figure of his day:
Of how he fought, fished, hunted, worked all night,
Though giddy, climbed new mountains; named a sea:
Some of the last researchers even write
Love made him weep his pints like you and me.

With all his honours on, he sighed for one
Who, say astonished critics, lived at home;
Did little jobs about the house with skill
And nothing else; could whistle; would sit still
Or potter round the garden; answered some
Of his long marvellous letters but kept none.

Brussels in Winter

Wandering through cold streets tangled like old string,
Coming on fountains rigid in the frost,
Its formula escapes you; it has lost
The certainty that constitutes a thing.

Only the old, the hungry and the humbled
Keep at this temperature a sense of place,
And in their misery are all assembled;
The winter holds them like an Opera-House.

Ridges of rich apartments loom to-night
Where isolated windows glow like farms,
A phrase goes packed with meaning like a van,

A look contains the history of man,
And fifty francs will earn a stranger right
To take the shuddering city in his arms.

Rimbaud

The nights, the railway-arches, the bad sky,
His horrible companions did not know it;
But in that child the rhetorician's lie
Burst like a pipe: the cold had made a poet.

Drinks bought him by his weak and lyric friend
His five wits systematically deranged,
To all accustomed nonsense put an end;
Till he from lyre and weakness was estranged.

Verse was a special illness of the ear;
Integrity was not enough; that seemed
The hell of childhood: he must try again.

Now, galloping through Africa, he dreamed
Of a new self, a son, an engineer,
His truth acceptable to lying men.

JAMES REEVES

Rough Weather

To share with you this rough, divisive weather
And not to grieve because we have to share it,
Desire to wear the dark of night together
And feel no colder that we do not wear it,
Because sometimes my sight of you is clearer,
The memory not clouded by the sense,
To know that nothing now can make you dearer
Than does the close touch of intelligence,
To be the prisoner of your kindnesses
And tell myself I want you to be free,
To wish you here with me despite all this,
To wish you here, knowing you cannot be—
This is a way of love in our rough season,
This side of madness, the other side of reason.

Delirium in Vera Cruz

Where has tenderness gone, he asked the mirror
Of the Biltmore Hotel, cuarto 216. Alas,
Can its reflection lean against the glass
Too, wondering where I have gone, into what horror?
Is that it staring at me now with terror
Behind your frail tilted barrier? Tenderness
Was here, in this very bedroom, in this
Place, its form seen, cries heard, by you. What error
Is here? Am I that rashed image?
Is this the ghost of the love you reflected?
Now with a background of tequila, stubs, dirty collars,
Sodium perborate, and a scrawled page
To the dead, telephone off the hook? In rage
He smashed all the glass in the room. (Bill: $50.)

GEORGE BARKER

To my Mother

Most near, most dear, most loved and most far,
Under the window where I often found her
Sitting as huge as Asia, seismic with laughter,
Gin and chicken helpless in her Irish hand,
Irresistible as Rabelais, but most tender for
The lame dogs and hurt birds that surround her,—
She is a procession no one can follow after
But be like a little dog following a brass band.

She will not glance up at the bomber, or condescend
To drop her gin and scuttle to a cellar,
But lean on the mahogany table like a mountain
Whom only faith can move, and so I send
O all my faith, and all my love to tell her
That she will move from mourning into morning.

When all my five and country senses see

When all my five and country senses see,
The fingers will forget green thumbs and mark
How, through the halfmoon's vegetable eye,
Husk of young stars and handfull zodiac,
Love in the frost is pared and wintered by,
The whispering ears will watch love drummed away
Down breeze and shell to a discordant beach,
And, lashed to syllables, the lynx tongue cry
That her fond wounds are mended bitterly.
My nostrils see her breath burn like a bush.

My one and noble heart has witnesses
In all love's countries, that will grope awake;
And when blind sleep drops on the spying senses,
The heart is sensual, though five eyes break.

JOHN BERRYMAN

I wished, all the mild days of middle March

I wished, all the mild days of middle March
This special year, your blond good-nature might
(Lady) admit—kicking abruptly tight
With will and affection down your breast like starch—
Me to your story, in Spring, and stretch, and arch.
But who not flanks the wells of uncanny light
Sudden in bright sand towering? A bone sunned white.
Considering travellers bypass these and parch.

This came to less yes than an ice cream cone
Let stand . . . though still my sense of it is brisk:
Blond silky cream, sweet cold, aches: a door shut.
Errors of order! Luck lies with the bone,
Who rushed (and rests) to meet your small mouth, risk
Your teeth irregular and passionate.

Concord

Ten thousand Fords are idle here in search
Of a tradition. Over these dry sticks—
The Minute Man, the Irish Catholics,
The ruined bridge and Walden's fished-out perch—
The belfry of the Unitarian Church
Rings out the hanging Jesus. Crucifix,
How can your whited spindling arms transfix
Mammon's unbridled industry, the lurch
For forms to harness Heraclitus' stream!
This Church is Concord—Concord where Thoreau
Named all the birds without a gun to probe
Through darkness to the pained man and bow:
The death-dance of King Philip and his scream
Whose echo girdled this imperfect globe.

The North Sea Undertaker's Complaint

Now south and south and south the mallard heads,
His green-blue bony hood echoes the green
Flats of the Weser, and the mussel beds
Are sluggish where the webbed feet spanked the lean
Eel grass to tinder in the take-off. South
Is what I think of. It seems yesterday
I slid my hearse across the river mouth
And pitched the first iced mouse into the hay.
Thirty below it is. I hear our dumb
Club-footed orphan ring the Angelus
And clank the bell-chain for St Gertrude's choir
To wail with the dead bell the martyrdom
Of one more blue-lipped priest; the phosphorus
Melted the hammer of his heart to fire.

Charles the Fifth and the Peasant
(after Valéry)

Elected Kaiser, burgher and a knight,
Clamped in his black and burly harness, Charles
Canters on Titian's sunset to his night;
A wounded wolfhound bites his spurs and snarls:
So middle-aged and common, it's absurd
To picture him as Caesar, the first cause
Behind whose leg-of-mutton beard, the jaws
Grate on the flesh and gristle of the Word.

The fir trees in the background buzz and lurch
To the disgruntled sing-song of their fears:
'How can we stop it, stop it, stop it?' sing
The needles; and the peasant, braining perch
Against a bucket, rocks and never hears
His Ark drown in the deluge of the King.

GIL ORLOVITZ

In negligent stone

In negligent stone the old man superintends
his vanishing; it is clear I am his son.
No longer will you take issue, he offends
me at the ark; you and I go one by one.
I may wave in a kind of offhand disaster,
but my prowl upon the limits done
though slow in grief in death is faster,
my father more to come, myself to shun.
I cry for an empty socket in the dark
if there be an eye for an eye. There's none:
I must take revenge out upon my own stark
self, and let fevers, like children, run
run into the earth and count with him how
we number neither more nor less than now.

JOHN HEATH-STUBBS

Hart Crane

The green-wombed sea proves now a harsher lover
And more acquisitive than her easy sons,
As furtively the crab, her agent, scans
The inventory of heart and brain and liver;

You suffer here, beyond the plunge of diver,
Her deeper perfidies: the warm stream runs
With gifts of boughs and birds, dead Indians
To each fresh voyager; yet still, deceiver,

Her laced white fingers lap a hollow land,
Where with false rhetoric through the hard sky
The bridges leap, twanged by dry-throated wind,

And crowded thick below, with idiot eye
The leaning deadmen strive to pierce the dim
Tunnels and vaults, which agate lamps illume.

DAVID WRIGHT

Wordsworth

There is a cragbound solitary quarter
Hawk's kingdom once, a pass with a tarn
High on its shoulder. Inscribed on a stone
With graveyard letters, a verse to his brother
Says it was here they parted from each other
Where the long difficult track winding down
A bald blank bowl of the hills may be seen
Leading the eye to a distant gleam of water.
After that last goodbye and shake of the hand
A bright imagination flashed and ended;
The one would live on, for forty years becalmed
Among the presences he had commanded—
Those energies in which the other foundered,
Devoured by wind and sea in sight of land.

E.P. at Westminster

Old whitebearded figure outside the abbey,
Erect, creating his own solitude,
Regards, tremulously, an undistinguished crowd,
Literati of the twentieth century.
They have come to pay homage to his contemporary;
He, to a confederate poet who is dead.
The service is over. Fierce and gentle in his pride,
A lume spento, senex from America,

He can only remember, stand, and wonder.
His justice is not for us. The solitary
Old man has made his gesture. Question now
Whom did the demoded Muse most honour
When she assigned with eternal irony
An order of merit and a cage at Pisa?

PHILIP LARKIN

The Card-Players

Jan van Hogspeuw staggers to the door
And pisses at the dark. Outside, the rain
Courses in cart-ruts down the deep mud lane.
Inside, Dirk Dogstoerd pours himself some more,
And holds a cinder to his clay with tongs,
Belching out smoke. Old Prijk snores with the gale,
His skull face firelit; someone behind drinks ale,
And opens mussels, and croaks scraps of songs
Towards the ham-hung rafters about love.
Dirk deals the cards. Wet century-wide trees
Clash in surrounding starlessness above
This lamplit cave, where Jan turns back and farts,
Gobs at the grate, and hits the queen of hearts.

Rain, wind and fire! The secret, bestial peace!

In a Garden

When the gardener has gone this garden
Looks wistful and seems waiting an event.
It is so spruce, a metaphor of Eden,
And even more so since the gardener went,

Quietly godlike but, of course, he had
Not made me promise anything and I
Had no-one tempting me to make the bad
Choice. Yet I still felt lost and wonder why.

Even the beech tree from next door which shares
Its shadow with me, seemed a kind of threat.
Everything was too neat and someone cares

In the wrong way. I need not have stood long
Mocked by the smell of a mown lawn, and yet
I did. Sickness for Eden was so strong.

IAIN CRICHTON SMITH

Orpheus

I

And he said, I am come in search of her
bringing my single bitter gift. I have
nothing more precious to offer
than this salt venom seeming to you as love.
It is true I cannot live without her
since I am now shade who was once fire.
See, mineral spirit, how I now suffer
by the slow heavy motion of my lyre.

And the god then replying, Let her stay
for by her absence your music is more clear,
barer and purer. Always in the air
her distance will perfect her as Idea.
Better the far sun of an April day
than fleshly thunder in the atmosphere.

2

And he said, That is great condemnation,
to live profoundly and yet much alone.
To see deeply by a barren passion.
It was forgetfully I moved the stone
which now submits to my examination.
She was my sense; around her flowing gown
my poems gathered in their proper season.
They were her harvest yet they were my own.

And the god then replying, What you say
is what her absence taught you. Our return
is not permissible to an earlier way.
If it were possible you would learn to mourn
even more deeply. Do you never burn
poems whose language was becoming gray?

3

And he to the god, If you should let her go
I'd know my music had its former power
to melt you too as once it melted snow
to alter you as once it altered her
so that in music we both learned to grow.
It was a dance of earth and of the air.
But up above it's easier. Here below—
The shade then smiled and said, Behold her there,
and he beheld her whitely where she stood
in that deep shade. She seemed not to have changed
nor he to have changed either as he played.
And yet her apparition was so strange.
She didn't fit the music that he made.
The notes and she were mutually disarranged.

4

And the god to him, Now I must tell you clear
what you refuse to see, since it is hard
to accuse ourselves of cruelty and fear.
You wished that she would die. And what you heard
was not my voice but yours condemning her.
If you will learn to love you must go forward.
For that is how it is in the upper air.
All that you have shared you have now shared.

And Orpheus took his lyre and left that place
and moved where the shadows moved and the clouds flowed
and all that lived had its own changing grace.
As on an April day there was sun and shade
but nothing vicious or virtuous
haunted the various music that he played.

GEOFFREY HILL

Requiem for the Plantagenet Kings

For whom the possessed sea littered, on both shores,
Ruinous arms; being fired, and for good,
To sound the constitution of just wars,
Men, in their eloquent fashion, understood.

Relieved of soul, the dropping-back of dust,
Their usage, pride, admitted within doors;
At home, under caved chantries, set in trust,
With well-dressed alabaster and proved spurs
They lie; they lie; secure in the decay
Of blood, blood-marks, crowns hacked and coveted,
Before the scouring fires of trial-day
Alight on men; before sleeked groin, gored head,
Budge through the clay and gravel, and the sea
Across daubed rock evacuates its dead.

Index of First Lines